PRATIHĀRENDURĀJA'S CONTRIBUTION TO SANSKRIT POETICS

PRATIHĀRENDURĀJA'S CONTRIBUTION TO SANSKRIT POETICS

ANITA KARA

Eastern Book Linkers
DELHI : : (INDIA)

Published by :
EASTERN BOOK LINKERS
5825, New Chandrawal, Jawahar Nagar,
Delhi-110007

First Edition : 1988

Price Rs. 150-

Sham Printing Agency (Amar Printing Press),
1/ε6A, Double Storey, Vijay Nagar, Delhi-110009

DEDICATED

TO

Mrs. Niharika
(my ma)

&

Mr. J. Karan
(my baba)

—*Author*

FROM ME......

After getting encouragement and mental preparation I started to write which is originally the result of my M. Phil research work. I joined the M. Phil course in 1984 in the University of Delhi. Before that I did my M.A. in Sanskrit from Utkal University. Earlier I specialised in Sanskrit Grammar but after happened meeting Prof. B.M. Chaturvedi, the Present Head of the Department of Sanskrit, University of Delhi, I made up my mind to take Poetics for M. Phil research work. It was all due to his valuable suggestions and encouragement in selecting my field as well as the topic. Of course, though it was a new field, it gave me immense pleasure and I am doing my Ph. D. work in the same field.

Poetics, a branch dealing with Poetry is concerned with several theories bearing upon sound and meaning also having affinity with Sanskrit Grammar, Mimansā, Philosophy and Nyāya etc.

I am deeply indebted to Dr. N.S. Shukla for his invaluable guidance at every stage of my work. Words are inadequate to express my gratitude to Prof. B. M. Chaturvedi for very cordial discussion about the topic from top to bottom. I am thankful to Prof. R.V. Joshi for his blessings Mrs. Sundari Siddhartha and Mr. Raman Kumar Sharma's help is really worthwhile to me.

My sincere thanks are due to the staff of central Reference Library, University of Delhi, Seminar Library, University of Delhi, Central secretariat Library, Delhi, for allowing me free access to their materials. Ms. Madhu, Eva, Surendra also deserve thanks for their help.

I am deeply thankful to Eastern Book Linkers, for the excellent Production of the book.

Finally, but not the least I must mention my Parents, brothers and sisters and my dadoo, Vijay uncle and Sana Kākā, & Bhanja Mausa who gave me all kinds of support to choose carrier in academic life.

(Visuva Samkranti)

ANITA KARAN

INTRODUCTION

(The present work is a culmination to the work which was originally submittcd to the University of Delhi as an M. Phil thesis in 1985).

The existence of two different Schools of rhetorics who accept the primacy of 'Vyangya-artha' and 'Abhivyakti Prakāra' is earned by the available works in the tradition of Indian poetics. Audicya and Dākṣiṇātya scholars represent these respectively which can be seen as the developed forms of the doctrine of 'contents' and 'From' in the modern technique of poetics. Bhāmaha has been the chief exponent of the former school, while Daṇḍin and Vāmana have represented the latter. Udbhaṭa is related to the Kashmiri School, He has borrowed a lot from Bhāmaha. Yet, sometimes he shows the different opinion by his originality and he strengthens that differences with minute observation. Udbhaṭa's independent and original evaluative style had an impact on Mammaṭa, Ruyyaka and later rhetoricians. In fact having touch to Udbhata, the alaṃkāra theory grew and established as Rasa and Dhvani in later stage.

In view of this, the position of Indurāja is somewhat unique. He had gone to Kashmir for studies. He learnt poetics from Mukulabhaṭṭa there. Yet, his interest for the Southern tradition is reflected in the Laghuvṛtti. He wrote a commentary on a Kashmiri work in the light of the ideas of the Southern Poetician, Vāmana. Consequently, a study of his work becomes more important of modern days.

Indurāja earned his good name as a commentator and also he came forth as a glistening star in the galaxy of alaṃkāra for strengthening the position of the figures of speech much above the realm of Dhvani which had obviously impressed the minds of the wise. Though Laghuvṛtti is not an independent work still it is highlighting the importance of Indurāja and his commentary remained always a lacuna as the critical and appreciative works found in the field of rhetorical literature.

The present work is a humble attempt to fulfil the want of research on Indurāja.

Secondly, Udbhaṭa has evaluated only alaṃkāras in his Kāvyālaṁkāra-Sāra-Saṃgraha. While evaluating it Indurāja has also discussed the intra-associated characteristics of Kāvya, Guṇa, Rasa and Dhvani. By his time, the Dhvani theory had also been well established Indurāja's originality lies in integrating it into the province of alaṃkāras.

First of all, chapter I has been devoted to a discussion of the development of the alaṃkāra concept alongwith the Early History of Alaṃkaras till Indurāja to enable to understand the position of Udbhaṭa etc. and Indurāja in the alaṃkāra atmosphere.

Chapter II gives a brief Introduction about the author, Udbhaṭa and his commentators. The originality of this chapter lies in relating the available information of Pratihārendurāja and Bhaṭṭendurāja to Indurāja and proved their identity by studying it as a whole.

Chapter III consists of the Treatment of Guṇa, Rasa, Dhvani according to the concept of Indurāja.

Chapter IV the Advent of the word 'Alaṁkāra' in Sanskrit Poetics' is mentioned along with the Analytical study of Kāvyālaṃkāra-Sāra-Saṃgraha with Laghuvṛtti in the light of literary analysis.

In Conclusion a brief arrangement of the ideas in the field of knowledge about the contribution of Laghuvṛttikāra, his identity and the position and development of alaṃkāras since remote past is discussed.

ANITA KARAN

ABBREVIATIONS

Comm.	...	Commentary
ed.	...	edition
HSP	...	History of Sanskrit Poetics
KASS	...	Kāvyālaṃkāra-Sāra-Saṁgraha
MSS.	...	Manuscripts
SV	...	Sāma Veda
VS	...	Vikram saṃvat
अ० गु०	...	अभिनवगुप्त
अ० वृ० मा०	...	अभिधावृत्त मातृका
अ० श०	...	अमरूशतक
अ० स०	...	अलंकार सर्वस्व
ए०	...	एकावली
औ० वि० च०	...	औचित्य विचार चर्चा
का० अ०	...	काव्यालंकार (भामह)
का० अ० (रु०)	...	काव्यालंकार (रुद्रट)
का० अ० टी०	...	काव्यालंकार टीका
का० अनु०	...	काव्यानुशासन
का० आ०	...	काव्यादर्श
का० प्र०	...	काव्यप्रकाश
का० प्र० सं०	...	काव्यप्रकाश संकेत
का० मी०	...	काव्यमीमांसा
का० सा० सं०	...	काव्यालंकार-सार-संग्रह
का० सू० वृ०	...	काव्यालंकार सूत्र वृत्ति
घ० क० कू० टी०	...	घटकर्परकूलकटीका

ध्व० आ०	...	ध्वन्यालोक
ध्व० लो०	...	ध्वन्यालोकलोचन
ना० शा०	...	नाट्यशास्त्र
नि०	...	निरुक्त
प्र० रु० य० भू० टी०	...	प्रतापरुद्रीययशोभूषण टीका
भ० का०	...	भट्टि काव्य
भ० गी० टी०	...	भगवद्गीताटीका
म० भा०	...	महाभारत
रा० त०	...	राजतरङ्गिणी
ल० वि०	...	लघु विवृति
ल० वृ०	...	लघु वृत्ति
वि० टी०	...	विमर्शिनी टीका
व्य० वि० टी०	...	व्यक्ति विवेक टीका
शृ० प्र०	...	शृङ्गार प्रकाश
सु० आ०	...	सुभाषितावली
सु० ति०	...	सुवृत्ततिलक
सं० श० कौ०	...	संस्कृत शब्द कौस्तुभ

CONTENTS

CHAPTER I

THE EARLY HISTORY OF ALAṀKĀRA

The first reference of the word 'Upamā' is found in the Nirukta, where its use is attested by Gārgya.[1] It was during the period of Bharata, that 'Upamā' obtained its prime position among the prevalent four major alaṃkāras which came into existence. The history of alaṃkāra goes into oblivion during a considerable gap in between Bharata and Bhāmaha. However, we come across references of some of the alaṁkāras during this time by some little-known rhetoricians. Alaṃkāra was only known as a branch of the Nātya Śāstra before Bhāmaha. It is from Bhāmaha that we infer that he studied his predecessors, especially Medhāvin, the prominent rhetorician, who dealt with seven Upamā-doṣas[2] and the Yathāsaṁkhya[3] Alaṃkāra.

An account of Medhāvin is also found in Namisādhu,[4] the commentator of Rudrata's Kāvyālaṃkāra. Vidyādhara in his

---

१. यदतत्रत्सदृशमिति गार्ग्यः । तदासां कर्म ।

—यास्क, नि० ३।१३, पृ० १६२

२. एत त उपमादोषाः सप्त मेघाविनोदिताः ।
सोदाहरण लक्ष्माणी वर्ण्यन्ते त्र च ते पृथक् ॥

—का० अ० २।४०

३. यथासंख्यमयौत्प्रेक्षामलङ्कार इयं विदुः ।
संख्यानमिति मेघाविनीत्प्रेक्षाभिहिता क्वचित् ॥

—क० अ० २।८८

४. ननु सन्त्येव दण्डिमेधा विरुद्ध भामहादिकुतानि अलङ्कार शास्त्रं ग्रन्थानि । —नमिसाधु, का० अ० टी० १-२

५. पूर्वेभ्यो भामहादिभ्यः सादरं विहिताञ्जलिः ।

—विद्याधर, का० अ० १।२

Ekāvali[5] mentions old poeticians along with Bhāmaha and Daṇḍin.

The number of alaṃkāras continued on the rise and we find Bharata mentioning four alaṃkāras in his Nātya Śāstra.[6] The number of alaṃkāras extended from one to four during the time of Bharata, the enunciator of Rasa School. He elaborately mentions about the salient points of the Nātya Śāstra and the concept of Rasa where he casually deals with alaṃkāras. Very often during that time, the rhetoricians used the epithet of 'Śovā', 'Vakratā', 'Saundarya' 'Cārutva' and Alaṃkāra for the embellishment of the Kāvya. However the name 'alaṃkāra' (अलङ्कार संज्ञा) become most popular among the poeticians and thus a new name of Alaṃkāra Śāstra was given to the Śāstra which thus evolved.

Coming back to this apparently dark period of alaṃkāra (between Bharata and Bhāmaha) we come across the first reference of 'Anuprāsa' mentioned by one 'Pracetāyana'.[7] The alaṃkāravādins concentrated assiduously on the establishment of the alaṃkāras throughout the age. It is seen in the introductory chapter of Kāvya-Mimāṁsā, a list about the figures

---

५. उपमारूपकं चैवदीपकं यमकं तथा ।
अलंकारास्तु विज्ञेयाश्चत्वारो नाटकात्रयाः ।।

—भरत, ना० शा० १६।४०

७. आनुप्रासिकं प्रचेतायनः, राजशेखर, का० मी०, अध्याय १, पृ० १

८. यमकं यमः, चित्रं चित्राङगदः, शब्दश्लेषशेषः, वास्तवं पुलस्त्यः, औपम्यमौपकायनः, अतिशयंपराशरः, अर्थश्लेषमुतथ्यः, उभयालंकारिकं कुबेरः । राजशेखर, का० मी, अध्याय प्रथम, पृ० १-२.

contributed by different poeticians of the hoary past.[9] It is thus found in the Kāvya Mimāṃsā that the Śabda Śleṣa was put forth by Śeṣa, Vāstava was by Pulastya, Aupamya Mūlaka by Aupakāyana. Even before Bharata, the Yamakālaṃkāra was introduced by Āchārya Yama, and further that Atiśaya, Arthaśleṣa, Udbhayālaṁkāra were invented by Parāśara, Uthaya and Kuber respectively.

By this lone contributions of each rhetorician, the slendar body of alaṃkāra boosted up and some of these remained hidden in the body of other alaṃkāras and could not come up independently in the coming up of the alaṃkāra literature.

The number later increased by the unstinted support of Viṣṇu-Dharmottara Purāṇa. The Viṣṇu-Dharmottara Purāṇa points out in the pauranic vein and sends the alaṁkāra into a state of multiplication. By this time, the alamkāras thus reach the number eighteen.[9] An indicatian of 38 alaṃkāra is found in the Bhaṭṭi-Kāvya.[10]

Even when a legacy of alaṁkāras could have been there before Bhāmaha, it is in him alone that we find an early exponent of the alaṁkāra school. The contribution of Bhāmaha is highly esteemed and influential in the whole

---

९. अनुप्रास ३ १४.१, यमक ३.१४.२३, रूपक ३.१४.४, व्यतिरेक ३.१४.५, श्लेष ३.१४.६, उत्प्रेक्षा ३.१४.७, उपन्यास ३.१४.९, अर्थान्तरन्यास ३.१४ ८, विभावना ३.१४.१०, अतिशयोक्ति ३.१४.२० स्वभावोक्ति ३.१४.११, यथासंख्या ३.१४.११-१२, विशेषोक्ति ३ १४.१२, विरोध ३.१४.१३, निन्दास्तुति ३.११.१३-१४, निदर्शना ३.१४.१४, उपमा ३.१४.१५, अनवय ३.१४.१५ ।

—वि० ध० पु० ३।१४

१०. भट्टि, भ० का०, दशम सर्ग

rhetoric atmosphere. He has clearly stated that the alaṁkāras are the ornaments,[11] but he is rigid on this point that these should be Vakrokti-Mūlaka or based on Vakrokti[12]. The theory of the Vakrokti has been found an improvement in his hands as he recognises the strikingness of 'Vakrokti' in alaṁkāras. After him, the name of Chitrāṅgada[13] came into existence for his contribution of Chitrālaṁkāra.

After Bhāmaha, we come across the well-known critic and poet Daṇḍin in the field of poetics who flourished in 700 A.D. He wins credit for his more systematic presentation of the alaṁkāras and their doctrine which produces the poetic beauty[14] and enhances it into an awakening sense with wider application. When he speaks of guṇa he alludes those qualities also which bring out the inherent beauty of poetry. Daṇḍin says that Prasāda etc. are the 'Viśeṣa alaṁkāras' and Upamā etc. are the 'sādhāraṇa alaṃkāras'. The Viśeśa alaṃkāras described by him at the time of Mārga-Vibhāga.[15]

Taking a clue from this statement of Daṇḍin, later rhetoricians distinguished the guṇas and alaṁkāras. Vāmana

---

११. न कान्तमपि निर्भूषं विभाति वनितानननम् ।
—का० अ० १।१३

१२. सैषा सर्वेव वक्रोक्तिरनयार्थो विभाव्यते ।
यत्नोऽस्याम् कविनाकार्यः कोऽलंकारोऽनयानिन ॥
—का० अ० २।८५

१३. चित्रं चित्राङ्गदः । राजशेखर, का० मी०, प्रथम अध्याय, पृ० १

१४. काव्यशोभाकरान् धर्मान् अलङ्कारान् प्रचक्षते ।
—दण्डी, का० अ० २.१

१५. काश्चिन्मार्गविभागार्थमुक्ताः प्रागण्यलंक्रियाः ।
साधारणमलंकार जातमन्यत् प्रदर्श्यते ॥
—दण्डी का० आ० १.३

also agrees on this point.[16] Daṇḍin incorporates both guṇas and alaṁkāras together in Sanskrit poetics.

Udbhaṭa's high command in the field of alaṁkāra Ś āstra was so much befitting that writers like Ānandavardhana[17], Abhinavagupta, Mahimbhaṭṭa,[18] Mammaṭṭa and Ruyyaka[19] continued to accord him much of respect for his eruditions of literary merit. He takes guṇa and alaṁkāra to be identical.[20] The pertinence of alaṁkāra eleveted by his polemic discussion also substained its number and importance in KASS by Udbhaṭa.

The contribution of Indūrāja in the field of Alaṁkāra is that, he has commented a Kashmirian āchārya Udbhaṭa's work KASS. By Indurāja's commentary we came to know that Udbhaṭa has written two more works namely, Kumāra-Saṁbhava and Bhāmaha Vivaraṇa which is already missing from our sight. Another remarkable point is that Indurāja suggests Dhvani is associated with Alaṃkāra.[21] so according to

---

१६. काव्यशोभायाः कर्त्तारो धर्मागुणाः ।
—वामन, का० सू० वृ० ३.१.२

१७. तत्रभवद्भिरुद्भटादिभिः ।
—आनन्दवर्धन, ध्व० आ०

१८. इह हि चिरन्तनैरलंकारतन्त्रप्रजापतिभिर्भट्टोद्भट प्रभृतिभिः शब्दार्थधर्मा एवालंकाराः प्रतिपादिता नाभिधाधर्माः ।।
—व्य० वि० टी०

१९. इह हि तावद्भामहोद्भट प्रभृतयश्चिरंन्तनालंकारकाराः ।।
—रुय्यक, अ० स०, पृ० २

२०. उद्भटादिभिस्तु गुणालंकाराणां प्रायशः साम्यमेव सूचितम् ।
—रुय्यक, अ० स०, पृ० ४

२१. एष्वेवालंकारेष्वन्तर्भावात् ।।
—इन्दुराज, ल० वृ० पृ. वर्ग ६

his opinion it is not necessary to speak about Dhvani thought it was well established before him, by the propounder Ānandavardhana, while discussing about the general characteristics of Kāvya, Indurāja takes the opponent idea from Vāmana, a southern āchārya and he also discusses the relative importance of guṇa, alaṃkāra, rasa, dhvani almost according to Vāmana's consideration.

It is evident that the growth of alaṁkāras was embarked upon by several illustrious rhetoricians and Indūrāja sparkles as adistinguished commentator who profusely serves to strengthen the exposition of alaṁkāras along with the relative importancc of guṇa, rasa and dhvani.

CHAPTER II

UDBHAṬA AND HIS COMMENTATORS

(a) *LIFE HISTORY OF UDBHAṬA*

The alaṁkāras assumed an elegant and outstanding position by the scholarly contribution of a prolific writer like Udbhaṭa. The credit of the KASS is the touch stone of his literary merit which enchants the enlightened reader. This prominent āchārya was born and bred in Kashmir and was the chief of the Kashmir king Jayapiḍa's court. Esteemed āchārya Vāmana also got ministrial position during that time along with the poet Manoratha, Saṁkhadatta, Cataka and Sandhimāṇa in the saml court.[2] In the post-Bhāmaha period, Udbhaṭa scintillates as a living and adroit rhetorician. The capability of Udbhaṭa is so admirable that Ānandavardhana despite belonging to the other school pointedly refers to him as a venerable elderly author.[3] The Rājataranginī of Kalhaṇa mentions the perfect granduer of both Udbhaṭa and Ānanda-vardhana and further stipulates that Udbhaṭa belonged to the

---

१. विद्वान्दीनारलक्षेण प्रत्यहं कृतवेतनः ।
भट्टोद्भटस्तस्य भूमिभर्तुः सभापतिः ।
—कल्हण, रा० त. ४.४९५

२. मनोरथः शंखदत्तश्चटकः संधिमान् तथा ।
बभूवुः कवयस्तस्य वामनाद्याश्चमंत्रिणः ॥
— कल्हण, रा. त. ४.४९७

३. अन्यत्र वाच्यत्वेन प्रसिद्धौ यो रूपकादिलंकारः सोन्यत्र प्रतीयमानतया-
बाहुल्येन प्रदर्शित-स्तत्र भवद्भि भट्टोद्भटादिभिः ।
—आनन्दवर्धन, ध्व. आ.

reign of Jayāpiḍa (A.D. 779-813)[4] and Ānandavardhana attained celebrity during the reign of Avantivarman (A.D. 857-884).[5]

(b) *DESCRIPTION ABOUT THE MSS. OF KASS.*

These are the following Mss. and editions available for the KASS. :

DECCAN COLLEGE MSS.

This Ms. is named as Udbhaṭālaṁkāra Laghutīkāsahita. It was brought for the Mss. Library by Dr. G. Buhler in his tour for the search of Sanskrit Mss. in India. This number is 64 of 1873-74 collection at the Deccan College Mss, Library. Now it is deposited at the B. O. R. I. Poona. This Ms. was obatained at Jeasalmir in his tour of 1973-74. It īs faīrly legible and bold Nāgarī scripts. It contains 62 folios with 26 lines on each folio written on one side only. It begins :

।।नमो वीतरागाय ।। यल्लक्ष्म्या हसितैः सितैर्धवलितं । and ends in this manner—काव्यालङ्कारसारे लघुविवृतिमधात् कौङ्कणः श्रीन्दुराजः ।। मङ्गलं महाश्रीः ।।

N. D. Banhaṭṭi's edition (1925) is mainly based on thīs Ms.

GOVERNMENT MSS. LIBRARY, MADRAS

Another Ms. containing Udbhaṭa's text and a commentary different from that of Indurāja is deposited in the Government Mss. Library. Madras. This is a transcript from the original. Paper $10\frac{7}{8} \times 9\frac{1}{8}$. Foll. 34. lines 20 in a page. Devanagari. good.

---

४. कल्हण, रा. त. ४४९५

५. मुक्ताकणः शिवस्वामी कविरानन्दवर्धनः ।
प्रथो रत्नाकरश्चागात् साम्राज्येऽवन्तिवर्मणः ।।
—कल्हण, रा. त. ५.३४

Transcribed in 1919-20 from a Ms. of M.R. Ray, Nerayana Nambudripad, Kudalur Maha, Nareri, Malabar Dt. Folios la to 336, Folio 34 is left blank contains vargas 1 to 6 complete."

It is also evidently noted that the text with Pratihārendurāja's commentary is edited by M.R. Telang, Nirṇaya Sāgar Press, 1905, 1915 available in 1915 आदर्श पुस्तकपुण्य पत्तनस्थ राजकीय Library.

The edition of N. D. Banhaṭṭi with the commentary of Pratihārendurāja, by Bombay Sanskrit Series, Poona, 1925 is available. Then the 2nd edition was published by B.O.R.I. in 1982.

Rājānaka Tilaka wrote one commentary named Laghuvivṛti. This is found in Gaekwad Series No. 55. This commentary is critically edited with Introduction and Indexes by K. S. Rāmaswāmi Śāstri Śiromani in 1931 by Oriental Institute Baroda.

(c) *COMMENTARY ON KASS. OF RĀJĀNAK TILAK*

Though handy, the gloss of Rājānak Tilaka facilitates to procure a relevant discussion on KASS. He tries to improve upon the whole task in a more polished and consistent way which reflects his thoughtful penetration. When Tilaka explains the word वाचाम् mentioned in the Kārikā number 2 of the KASŚ, the explanation offered for this word, is 'word and its meaning', while other rhetoricians and commentators who preceded were of the opinion that it had only a restricted meaning of word alone. Also the treatment of Upamā-doṣas is considered a praiseworthy achievement where 21 varieties have been analysed by Tilaka. He glorifies the figure Upamā in a clearcut explanation. He stresses on the 'Samartha-Samarthaka relation' while commenting on the figure Arthāntarnyāsa and categorises it into 16 dissimilarities which clarify the author Udbhaṭa. In case of Vyatireka, Virodha and Aprastuta-prasaṁsā he also sufficiently justifies himself than the author. In preyas alaṁkāra Tilaka defines the 'Vyaṅgā-Vyaṅ janā' relation and establishes the importance of rasa in connection with Kāvya which accords him an extolled position in the field of alaṁkāra literature.

Ruyyaka composed 'Alaṁkāra sarvasva' in about A.D. 1150 where he mentions Rājānak Tilaka as his father.[8] It is thus clear that Rājānaka Tilaka flourished a little earlier than A.D. 1150. P.V. Kane establishes him in between A.D. 1100-1125.

The commentary Laghuvivṛtti is a brīef, elegant contribution by Tilaka. The commentator wants to defend in many places to Indurāja's opinion and stresses his own view and sometimes he also tries to refute the author. It is in compendīum form with full of meanings and orginality of Rājānak Tilaka.

(d) *THE KASS AND THE LAGHUVṚTTI*

The development of the alaṁkāra reaches a new apex in the treatise of Udbhaṭṭa entitled KASS. The whole work treats and accords 41 alaṁkāras into six groups. The order of the alaṁkāras is more scientific which supercedes the old achāryas due to their scanty knowledge. The KASS. bore an out-standing influence in the progressive province of alaṁkāras which is anxiously admired by the readers,

---

८. ज्ञात्वा श्रीतिलकात्सर्वालंकारोपनिषत्क्रमम् ।
काव्य प्रकाशसंकेतौ रूपकेनेह लिख्यते ॥
रूय्यक प्रणीतका प्र. स. मङ्गलाचरणम् quoted in 22 page ग्र. स. R. C. Dwivedi.

The commentary of KASS is very lucid and well-explained by Indurāja. In Laghuvṛtti, the commentator explains very apt explanation to the first group of alaṁkāras.

The second group treats of six alaṁkāras. In the third group there are only three figures. These order of enumeration follows to Bhāmaha. The fourth and fifth groups consist of the of Bhāmaha.

Then the last instalment of alaṁkāras neither agree with the enumeration of Bhāmaha nor Daṇḍin, of course it carries apparently similar to that of Bhāmaha, In this way the gloss, Laghuvṛtti strives to bring forth a number of alaṁkāras combined according to the proximity in the field of Sanskrit Literature and which is really appreciated by the enchanted readers,

(e) *PRATIHĀRENDURĀJA : THE LAGHUVṚTTIKĀRA*

According to the information available, the most striking sanskrit commentator of Kashmir in this age was Indurāja who flourished in the middle of A.D. 10. Even if his commentary is a strong footing to alaṁkāra literature he has not forgotten to discuss the rasa, guṇa, Dhvani and the general characteristics of poetry in the same way as Vāmana. He also did not establish the Dhvani theory though during his time the dhvani has its abiding effect as it achieved its proper importance. Indurāja does not appear to have written any independent work of his own still he has successfully commented the brief accounts of rasa, guṇa, alaṁkāra. He was not quite satisfied with Bhāmaha's description about Prasāda, Mādhurya, oajas so he established a midway accepting the guṇasvarūpa of vāmana and the number and guṇas Saṁjnās from Ānandavardhana. Indurāja is famous for his insight into the depth of the alaṁkāras as well as the Kāvya consideration.

He refers to the names like Bhāmaha, Udbhaṭa, Rudraṭa, Vāmana, Ānandavardhana and their profound knowledge.

(f) *PRATIHĀRENDURĀJA AND BHAṬṬENDURĀJA*

Given the nature of the chronology and historical data it has been impossible to reach a consensus regarding the identity of Indurāja. There is debate on whether one single individual or two different persons are indicated by the available data. Though the historicity of the real facts about Indurāja is enveloped by a number of reasons even then on the whole we can hold them as identical by considering the scattered data which available regarding him.

It is noteworthy that 'Samudrabandha,[7] on the Alaṁkāra-Sarvasva seems to identify the above two Indurājas by calling Pratihārendurāja by the name Bhaṭṭendurāja.

This shows the link between Bhaṭṭendurāja and Udbhaṭa which is indicated by the testimony supplied by the writing remains in Samudrabandha on Alaṁkāra-sarvasva. The synchronisms obtained from the independent sources as shown in Laghuvṛtti would strongly support the contention that the name Pratihārendurāja[8] Śrī Indurāja[9] and Mahāśrī Indurāja[10] is one

---

७. Reference found in HSP, P. V. Kane, pp. 206-7

८. विद्वदग्रथान्मुकुलकादधिगम्य विविच्यते ।
प्रतीहारेन्दुराजेन काव्यालंकारसंग्रहः ॥
—इन्दुराज, ल. वृ., पृ. १

९. श्रुत्वा सौजन्यसिन्धोर्द्विजवरमुकुलात्कीर्तिवल्क्यालभवालात् ।
काव्यालंकारसारे लघुविवृतिमघात्कौकणः श्रीन्दुराजः ॥
—इन्दुराज, ल. वृ., पृ० ८२

१०. (इति) महाश्रीप्रतीहारेन्दुराजविरचितायामुद्भटालंकार सार संग्रह-लघुवृत्तौ षष्ठोवर्गः ॥
—इन्दुराज ल. वृ. पृ ८२

and the same person. The samudrabandha has quoted the name of Bhaṭṭendurāja, who comments Udbhaṭṭa's work,[11] so thus on this basis we can say that Indurāja remembered with the prefixes 'Śrī', 'Mahāśrī, 'Pratihāra' and 'Bhaṭṭa' one and tree same personality and all the references available regarding Pratihārendurāja or Bhaṭṭendurāja or indurāja go to the same character. In this light the scholars who have considered and noticed them as separate substantially insufficient and insignificant. K.C. Pandey[12] also holds the view that the gloss on KASS written by Indurāja, who had the prefixes of the title Pratihāra, Bhaṭṭa and Śrī. At one place Abhinavugupta has quoted his preceptar,[13] without any title as only Indurāja in his commentary on Ghatakarparakūlaka. Mukunda Mādhava Sharma also considers in this regard in his book also.

Discussing the point regarding the title. Bhaṭṭa[14] means 'a respected person', 'learned teacher'. Abhinavagupta might have prefixed him as the title 'Bhaṭṭa' due to 'respect' and spelied him as Bhaṭṭendurāja.

In the reference of Indurāja's place the logical supposition would go as a support to the slender consideration of the scholars like P.V. Kane[15] and S.K. De. About his place we

---

११. भट्टेन्दुराजेन प्रीणित प्रणयीत्यादि अप्रस्तुतप्रशंसोदाहरणे ।

१२ के. सि. पाण्डे—अ. गु., पृ. २१३

१३. कबीन्दोराजस्य ते सद्धित्तबिकाशका: ।
वीघांशवौ विगाहन्तां भुर्भुवस्व:स्त्रयीमपि ।
घ.क. कू. टी , पृ० २१३

१४. भट्ट—सम्मानित विद्वान या अध्यापक की उपाधि, पृ० ८१८—
सं. श. कौ.

१५. Though भट्टेन्दुराज and प्रतीहारेन्दुराज were both of them well versed in Alaṁkāra Śāstra and flourished nearly at the same time, they must be regarded as distinct.

—P.V. Kane. H.S.P., p. 205

have considered that he was a Kaunkaṇa but he had gone to Kashmir for study. He was a disciple of Mukula there.[16] We donot know anything about the parentage of Pratihārendurāja and it is to be seen that Bhaṭṭendurāja belonged to Kātyāyana gotra and was son of Śrībhūtirāja and grandson of Saucuka[17]. This woutd suggest that he was the same person who belonged to the same gotra because it has been observed that the Kātyā-yana gotra is found in Mahārāstra[19] Brahmin family and Pratihārendurāja's native place was in Konkaṇa,[19] near Mahārāṣṭra. While tracing the question of Kātyāyana gotra which is related with Sāmaveda[20] also relates the title 'Pratihāra'. It only mean the particular syllables in the sāma-hymns which the Pratihartṛi has to sing.[21]

It is reasonable to assume that the above conclusion drawn of the identification accepted by scholars like Peterson,[22]

---

१६. विद्वदग्रयान्मुकुलकादधिगम्य विविच्यते ।
प्रतीहारेन्दुराजेन काव्यालंकारसंग्रहः ।।
—इन्दुराज-ल. वृ., प्रथम अध्याय, पृ १

१७. भट्टेन्दुराजादाम्नायं विविध च चिरं धिया कृतोऽभिनवमुक्ति । सोऽयं गीतार्थ संग्रहः ।
—अभिनवगुप्त, भगवद्गीताटीका, नि० सा० प्र. पृ० ६, श्लोक ६

१८. Quoted form संस्कृत व्याकरण का उद्भव और विकास, S.K. Varma, Page 181.

१९. श्रुत्वा सौजन्य सिन्धोर्द्विजवरमुकुलात्कीर्तिवल्यारुवालात् ।
काव्यालंकारसारे लघुविवृतिमघात्कौङ्कणः श्रीन्दुराजः ।।
—इन्दुराज, ल. वृ, पृ. ९२

२०. From N.D. Banahatti, p. xxvi

२१. Reference found in KASS with Laghuvṛtti in N.D. Banahatti. p. xxviii.

२२. Reference found in HSP. SK. De, p. 74.

K.C. Pandey, Kshemendra[23] which brings nearer to the establishment of the identific tion.

Himself a devotee of Guru Bhattendurāja, Abhinavagupta was placed with certainty at the last quarter of 10 th and first quarter of the eleventh century A.D. That is why it is fairly assigned that his Preceptor, Bhaṭṭendurāja must belong a bit earlier to him which can be consequently stated to be the middle of 10th century A.D. This also equates the chronology of Pratihārendurāja. It appears that the chronology of Mukulabhaṭṭa is assigned to A. D. 900-925[24] and this date brings us nearer to the establishment of his pupil, the Laghuvṛttikāra, Indurāja in the middle of the 10 century A.D. This is a fair conclusion regarding the chronological doubt. Also N.D. Banhatti in his Appendix V mentions Indurāja or Bhaṭṭendurāja or pratihārendurāja as the author of Laghuvṛtti.

In order to prove that Pratihārendurāja and Baṭṭendurāja are one and the same person the evidence from the Sāma Veda can be quoted. It can be shown that the epithet 'Pratihāra' and the 'Kātyāyana gotra' both of which can be located in the Sv. and they refer to the same person namely Indurāja. We also known that persons belonging to the Kātyāyana gotra were inhabitants of Konkaṇa. The connection of Indurāja with Konkaṇa is clear from the last verse in which he has referred to himself as Kaunkaṇa. From all this scattered evidence we are able to establish the identy of Indurāja.

---

२३. a. ग्रादायवारिपरितः..... च । क्षेमेन्द्र, ग्रौ. वि च.

b ग्राचार्य वडवानलः सभगवानाश्चर्यंमम्भोनिधि...श्रमः ।

२४. भटटकल्लट पुत्रेणमुकुलेन निरूपिता ।

सूरि प्रबोधनायेमभिधावृत्तिमातृका ।

मुकुलभट्ट, ग्र. वृ. मा. श्लोक १५

CHAPTER III

A TREATMENT OF GUṄA, RASA AND DHVANI BY INDURĀJA

A close study of the commentary of Indurāja indicates effectively an interesting discussion on the nature of Sanskrit poetry. guṇa, rasa and dhvani. The treatment of alaṃkāras, guṇa, rasa and dhvani which are the main tenets of discussion of the rhetorical works in Sanskrit, an evaluation of all these put before us the contribution of Indurāja on a high pedestal. When Udbhata appears on the horizon the range of alaṃkāras reach a bigger number but they were not dealt in the light of guṇa, rasa, dhvani in poetry. Before Indurāja, the dhvani theory was well-developed in the filament of Sanskrit poetics, and the Sahṛdayas had already started thinking about the supremacy of dhvani. It is strange that, Indurāja considers the context of guṇa, rasa. dhvani relatively while commenting upon Udbhata just after the establishment of Dhvani Theory.

The discussion of guṇa had continued since the remote past in the Kāvya Śāstra. From the oldest available literary work like Nātya Śāstra, we know that Bharata discussed the guṇa aspect in kāvya. Doṣa is considered as Bhāvātmaka and in its viparyaya,[1] yāmana agrees to the opposite of it, Guṇa is Bhāvātmaka and doṣa is Niṣedhātmaka.[2] Bharata considers

---

१. गुणविपर्ययादोषाम् । भरत, ना., शा., १७.६४

२. गुण विपर्ययात्मानो दोषाः ।।

—वामन, का. सू. वृ. २.१.१

that both guṇa and alaṁkāra are 'Rasasamasrāyatmaka' having equal importance in Kāvya. Bhāmaha introduces guṇa by a new consideration, classifying three guṇas instead of ten mentioned by Bharata. He simply mentions the Mādhurjya, ojas, and Prasāda[3] but does not name them as guṇas, none does he connect them in any way with Mārga. He designates Bhāvika as a 'Prabandha Viṣaya guṇa'[4] where he is defined guṇa. The KASS. of Udbhaṭa is a lucid work of figures of speech and has no place for guṇas. But his ideas on guṇas which is expressed in his lost commentary on Bhāmaha, quoted in the Ratnāpaṇa commentary on Pratāparūdriya[5]. Udbhaṭa states that there is essentially no difference between guṇa and alaṃkāra due to their beautifying quality in Kāvya.[6] And the distinction alleged to exist is due to the Saṁghatanāśrita of guṇa and Śabdārthāśrita of alaṁkāra.[7] Otherwise there is no difference between them. Raising this abedatva, Vāmana speaks that guṇa deals with 'Kāvyaśabhākāraka', and alaṃkāra as 'Kāvyaśobhātiśayakatva[8]

---

३. माधुर्यमभिवाञ्छन्तः प्रसादं च सुमेधसः ।
समासवन्ति भूयांसि न पदानि प्रयुञ्जते ॥
केचिदोजो भिधित्सन्तः समस्यन्ति बहून्यपि ॥
—का. अ., २.२-२

४. भाविकत्वमिति प्राहुः प्रबन्धविषयगुणम् ।
—का. अ. ३.५३

५. संघटनाश्रयाः गुणाः शब्दार्थाश्रयास्त्वलङ्कारा: ।
—रत्नापण टीका प्र. य. भू. २४४ विद्यानाथ

६. उद्भटादिभिस्तु गुणालंकाराणां प्रायंशः साम्यमेव सूचितम् ।
—रूय्यक : अ. स., पृ. ८

७. विषयमात्रैण भेद प्रतिपादनात् ।
—रूय्यक : अ. स., पृ. ८

८. काव्यशोभायाः कर्तारो धर्मागुणाः । तदतिक्रयहेतवस्त्वलंकाराः ।
—वामन, का. सू. वृ., ३.१.१-२

In the reference of poetry, Daṇdin has taken the guṇas to be the soul of Vaidarbha Mārga.[9] Daṇḍin's foremost acknowledgement on the position of guṇa is considered as its excellece of the poetry.

A drastic change came in the concept of guṇa when Dhvani theory formulated. The reason behind it. was, the aim of, rasa, to attain the poetic effect. While accepting the number of guṇas Indurāja follows the three guṇas spoken by Ānandavardhana i.e. Mādhurya, Ojas and Prasāda, though, he closely follows Vāmana on this issue. Indurāja makes himself as a fallower of Vāmana on the question of difference between guṇa and alaṃkāra and differs from Udbhaṭa in this respect. The fashioning of every part of the expression of the kāvya Śarīra needs rasa, guṇa and alaṃkāra. The vehicle of poetry is governed by Sārasatva[10] prasāda as the most important guṇa.[11] The guṇas are mentioned of three types i.e. Mādhurjya, Ojas and Prasāda.[12] According to Indurāja, Prasāda is the most essential guṇa for the expression of sentiments and it helps in the manifestation of the sentiments for poetry. Prasāda is stated by him for its 'Rasamūlakatā' and 'Rasa Niṣṭhatā'. which is the land-mark of his originality. Even if Indurāja's commen-

---

९. इति वैदर्भमार्गस्य प्राणा दशगुणाः स्मृताः ।

—दण्डी, का. आ., १.४२

१०. गुणसंस्कृतशब्दार्थशरीरत्वात्सरमेवकाव्यम् ।

—इन्दुराज, ल. वृ., ८३

११. तदेतेषां त्रयाणां गुणानां मध्यात्प्रसादस्य प्राधान्यम् ॥

—इन्दुराज, ल० वृ०, पृ० ८१

१२. गुणाः काव्यस्य माधुर्यौजः प्रसादलक्षणा ।

—इन्दुराज, ल० वृ०, पृ० ८१

tary basically meant only about alaṁkāras, still he has not forgotton to analyse about the guṇatrayavāda.

Prasāda is the major guṇa because it is the source of rasābhivyakti[13] and imparts importanee to the rasa. By associating with Mādhurya and Ojas and Prasāda[14] proceeds eternally assimilating the beauty of a kāvya and without guṇa there can be no Kāvyatva.[15] Alaṃkāras by themselves can add to the poetic effect and the absence of guṇas lessen the beauty of the Kāvya, which may also look ugly and inspid.[16] Indurāja quotes Vāmana on the distinction of guṇa and alaṁkāra and gives an example from the Amaruśataka[17] how guṇa can exist in poetry, without alaṃkāra[18]

He also defines Kāvya as Śabdārtha which beautifies by guṇas. Guṇa is a dharma of Śabdārtha. Kāvya will have a life

---

१३. प्रसादस्त्वव्यवधानेन रसाभिव्यक्त्यनुगुणता ।

इन्दुराज, ल० वृ०, पृ० ८१

१४. गुणरहितमकाव्यमकाव्यमेव भवति न त्वलङ्कारररहितम् ।

—इन्दुराज, ल० वृ०, पृ० ८२

१५. एवं च तत्र तदसानुशुण्येनमाधुर्योजोभ्यां तारतम्येनावस्थिताभ्यां उपकृती यो सो प्रासादात्मा रसानामव्यवधानेन । प्रतीतिहेतुर्गुणस्त-दुपेतशब्दार्थशरीरत्वेन काव्यस्यावस्थानात्सरसतैवभवति न तु नीरसता।

—इन्दुराज, ल० वृ०, पृ० ८१

१६. न खलु निर्गुणे काव्ये निबन्ध्यमानानामलङ्काराणां जरद्योषितदलङ्कार-वच्छ भि विधायित्वं दुश्यते ।

—इन्दुराज, ल० वृ०, पृ० ८१-८२

१७. अमरुशतक, श्लोक—७५-७८

१८. लक्ष्ये च अलङ्काररहितमपि केवलगुण सत्क्रियमाणशब्दार्थशरीरं काव्यं दृश्यते ।

—इन्दुराज, ल० वृ०, पृ० ८२

Jīvadrūpa)[19] only by possessing the soul of rasa. Indurāja separates rasa from its Śarīra which is Śabda and Artha. To this Śarīra belong the guṇas, Prasāda helped by Mādhurya and Ojas in a certain proportion, and such a Prasāda guṇa is the means of the manifestation of rasa.[20] Rasa is a subsidiary element in poetry. Rasa is nothing but the rasavat alaṃkāra itself.[21] Indurāja considers rasa as the soul of poetry where as Alaṁkāras are the soul of poetry in the treatment of Udbhaṭa.

Sometimes we come across the thoughts of logicians cited by Indurāja regarding the process of causation. This suggests that Indurāja also had knowledge about the Hetuvyāpāra. He includes his study on the eause and effect as the logicians view. In this way Indurāja's treatment of guṇa and rasa in Kāvya is very important and significant one.

Indurāja mentions the Dhvani theory of Ānandavardhana by saying that Dhvani is included in Alaṃkāras only.[22] Nowhere does he mention them by their names. He alludes to the successors of the dhvani theory by the title Sahṛdayas. These Sahṛdayas were a group of critics who criticised alaṃkāras and promulgated the dhvani theory in the field of

---

१९. यथा ह्यात्माधिष्ठितं शरीरं जीवतीति व्यपदिश्यते तथा रसाधिष्ठित-स्य काव्यस्य जीवद्रूपतया व्यपदेशः क्रियते तस्माद्रसानां काव्यशरीर-भूतशब्दार्थविषयतयात्मत्वेनावस्थानं नत्वलङ्कारतया ॥
—इन्दुराज, ल० वृ०, पृ० ८३

२०. रसाभिव्यक्तिश्च यथायोगं माधुर्यौजीभ्यां तारतम्येनावस्थिताभ्यामुप-बृंहिती योसो प्रसादात्मा गुणस्तेन क्रियते ।
—इन्दुराज, ल० वृ० पृ० ८३

२१. रसाः खलु तस्यालङ्कारः । —इन्दुराज, ल० वृ०, पृ० ५३

२२. एष्वेवालङ्कारेष्वन्तर्भावात् । —इन्दुराज, ल० वृ० पृ० ८५

Poetics. As the dhvani is included in alaṃkāra it has not been discussed separately according to Indurāja. There are three types of Dhvanis, viz. Vastudhvani. Alaṃkāradhvani and Rasadhvani.

In the first case Indurāja states to illustrate how th Vastudhvani is nothing but the Paryāyokta alaṃkāra[23] In case of Paryāyokta alaṃkāra the Vyaṅgyārtha is conveyed by the implication and by all those things which are wanted to be said.[24]

He clearly shows from the verse of the description of Viṣṇu.[25] Here the cause by which the love-sports were made futile is not expressed. The Rāhuśiraścchheda which is the cause of Cumbanamātraśeṣakaraṇa is understood by suggestion. The rāhu Śiraśchheda is neither a rasa nor the like, nor it is an alaṃkāra, it is simply a Vastumātradhvani, which goes under paryāyokta Alaṁkāra.

But the dispute arises regarding this argument. By the word 'Paryāyokta' is meant the thing that is implied. In this case the implication is the principal issue. That is why in the fitness of things it is a thing to be adorned (Alaṃkārya) and not an adornment (Alaṁkāra) itself.

The Siddhāntin replies that in some cases even the principal thing becomes the means of adorning, when it beauti-

---

२३. अतोत्र वस्तुमात्रश्चेवंविधस्य शब्दव्यापारास्पृष्टस्य प्रतीयमानता।

—इन्दुराज, ल० वृ०, पृ० ८६

२४. एवमन्यत्रापि वस्तुमात्रे प्रतीयमाने पर्यायोक्तता वाच्या ॥

—इन्दुराज, ल० वृ०, पृ० ८७

२५. चक्राभिघातप्रसभाज्ञयैव चकारयो राहुवधूजनस्य।
आलिङ्गनोद्दामविलासवन्ध्यं रतीसत्वं चुम्बनमात्र शेषम्।

—आनन्दवर्धन, ध्व० आ०; प्रथम उद्योत, पृ० ५४

fies the guṇas. It elevees the beauty of the subordinate sense Because sometimes it is seen that the assistants (bhṛtyas) are adorned by their lords only[26] In this way this Vastu can be said as alaṁkāra. The Paryāyokta alaṁkāra is not only concerned with other sentence but also with the word. Vastudhvani has been shown to be Paryāyokta alaṁkāra as the Padadhvani in the verse "Rāmosmic sarvamsahe". Indurāja states Paryāyokta alaṁkāra by accepting a group of Paryāyokta pertaining to a single word.[27]

The āropa of Candra upon mukha is implied in the example of Lābanyakanti etc. The implied alaṁkāra is Rūpaka but it should be Paryāyokta alaṁkāra in Indurāja's considera-tion in the sense of Vācyavācakaśūnya Avagamana Vyāpāra[18]. According to Ānandavardhana it is though the Rūpakadhvani still it is not a Rūpaka alaṁkāra because Dhvani is principal and Vācyartha is subordinate to it in the above example.

In the illustration of Suvarṇa Puṣpa etc. the Suvarṇa Puṣpa means bahulana and by the assistance of Lakṣaṇa the Dhvani is under stood. The Upamānopameyabhāva is evident in bahulā-bhatva and Suvarṇapuṣpatva, Śūra, Kṛtavidya and Mālākāra. Thus this impossibility brings forth the figure Vidarśanā.

---

२६. दृश्यते हि लोके व्यपदेशः स्वाभ्यलङ्करणकामृत्या इति ।

—इन्दुराज, ल० वृ०, पृ० ८६

२२. एत एव तु पयवाक्यप्रकाश्यतया द्वैमुप्यं.. ...आविर्भावात् ।

पदप्रकाश्यत्वं यथा रामोस्मीति, चक्राभिघातेत्यादौ तु वाक्य प्रकाश्यता ॥

—इन्दुराज, ल० वृ०, पृ० ९१

२८. तद्विषयस्य च काव्यधर्मस्य ध्वननाभिधानस्य वाच्यवाचकव्यापार-शून्यावगमनस्वभावत्वात्पर्यायोक्तालङ्कारसंस्पर्शित्वम् ।

—इन्दुराज, ल० वृ०; पृ० ८६

यथामालाकाराः सुवर्णपुष्पाणि चिन्वन्ति तथा शूराः बहुलाभां पृथिवीं प्राप्नुवन्ति ।

This example is called as Avivakśita Vācya Dhvani by Ānandavardhana. Here the Vācya yields place by Lakṣaṇa to bahulābhaprāpaṇa and from this the Vyaṅgyārtha is understood.

In this way Indurāja has explained these examples to prove that Alaṁkārarūpadhvani is included in the Alaṁkāras. He refutes the view point of Ānandavardhana, who reckoned Alaṁkāradhvani as a separate variety of Dhvani and did not include it under alaṁkāras which belong to the expressed sense only.

In the verse yātegotra Viparyaya etc. the Īrṣyāvipralaṁbha is conveyed by gotraviparyāya. The Saṁbhoga is the Pratīyamānortha and the cause of 'tirodhāna' or disappearance of Īrśyā Vipralaṁbha and saṁbhoga. Śṛṅgāra is known as Pratīya Mānortha,[21] which is also called the rasa Dhvani. this cause (Hetu) is known as Dhvanyatha. This is described as Rasavadalaṁkāra by Indurāja. This rasadhvani will also appear in other rasas,[30] where the pratiyamānasense is bhāva or Rasabhāvabhāsa or rasabhāvatadābhāsapraśama, there occurs the alaṁkāras like preyasvat, Ūrjasvi, Samāhita respectively. The subordinate to other rasas etc. or to the expressed sense, is known as the figure Udātta, which is based on the good deeds of great characters.

---

२६. अतोत्र संभोगश्रृङ्गारस्येर्ष्याविप्रलंभश्रृङ्गारातिरोधानहेतोः प्रतीयमानता ॥

—इन्दुराज, ल० वृ०, पृ० ८८

३०. एवं रसान्तरेष्वपिवाच्यम् ।

—इन्दुराज, ल० वृ०, पृ० ८८

Rasa has four stages, viz. rasa, bhāva, rasābhāsa/ Bhāvābhāsa and Rasapraśama bhāvapraśama. Bhāva is the brief stage of rasa and is the hiding and minute realisation whereas rasa is the revealed one. When rasa and bhāva is in principal one the rasvat, Preyasvat, Ūrjasvi and Samāhita alaṁkāras take place the figure and when it is in secondary sense the figure Udātta comes to this field. So there is essentially no necessity to suppose it as a separate dhvani.

In this way. Indurāja takes his stand on the tripod of rasa, alaṁkāra and guṇa intra-associated in the poetry. The rasas are the soul of poetry and words and sense are the body. Alaṁkāras are the ornaments of word and sense. So rasa cannot be used as the external ornament of the outer body. Kāvyas are Sarasa as contrasted with Śāstra. The rasa are the soul and life in whose absence the Kāvya is a corpse.

CHAPTER IV

ADVENT OF THE WORD 'ALAṀKĀRA' IN SANSKRIT POETICS

Vāmana clearly states the concept of dissimilarity of guṇa and alaṁkāra in a new way by proclaiming that the guṇas produce beauty in Kāvya and Alaṁkāras enhance it. According to these references before Vāmana Alaṁkāra was used in its narrow sense. Vāmana was aware of the broader meaning of this word which denotes the sum total of Sauṅdarya.[2] Daṇḍin also incorporates guna, Sandhyaṅgas. Vṛttyaṅgas, Lakṣaṇas etc.[3] while enunciating 'alaṁkāra'. He also strives to stress on the Upamā etc. Bhāmaha was the antagonist of the southern tradition, he was also an amplifier of the Kashmīri School. The major portion of his treatise is devoted to the discussion of alaṁkāras by which the denotation of Vakrokti is clothed as Arthavyutpatti,[4] Thus, there is a sweet relationship established in between Arthavyutpati and Alaṁkara which is already vakroktimūlaka. Thus, the life of Kāvya is alaṁkāra which is

---

१. काव्य शोभाया: कर्त्तारो धर्मा गुणा: ।
तदतिशय हेतवस्त्वलङ्कारा: । —वामन, का० सू० वृ० १ १.३

२. सौन्दर्यं अलङ्कार: । —वामन, का० सू० वृ० १.१.२

३. यच्च संध्यङ्ग वृत्यङ्ग लक्षणाद्यारामान्तरे ।
व्यावर्णितमिदं चेष्टमलङ्कारतयैव न: ॥
—दण्डी, का० आ०, २.३६७

४. सैषा सर्वैव वक्रोक्तिरणयार्थी विभाव्यते ।
यत्नो स्यां कविनां कार्य: कोऽलङ्कारौऽनया विना ॥
—भामह का० आ० २.८५

Vakroktimūlaka, and Vakratāhīnavākya is known as Vārtā[5]. This, theory is known as 'Vyaṅgyavāda', whereas the 'Sauśabda' is estadlished by southerners is called as 'Abhivyaktivāda'. Though Indurāja comments the alaṁkāra works of a Kashmirian āchārya still he adheres to the influence of Vāmana, a renowned rhetorician of southern tradition. Vāmana's brilliant analysis helps him as a stepping stone to sustain for immitating the well-nigh identity in the province of the word 'Alaṁkāra'. Udbhaṭa omits the general characteristics of alaṁkāra in his outstanding work KĀSS. He systematically starts about the definitions and illustrations of his six Vargas of alaṁkāras one by one In the hands of Indurāja the concept of alaṁkāra[6] receives an adroit recognition which is admixed with Vāman's declaration of poetry.[7] Vāmana says that the Kāvyasaundarya is generated by guṇas and elevated by alaṁkāras. This has been taken up by Indurāja.

Thus, the Southern Scholars emphasised on 'Padavinyāsa' and the Kashmirians on 'Arthavyutpati'. Inspite of the disparate tradition, both Bhāmaha[8] and Vāmana assigned equal importance regarding the characteristics of Kāvya. Bhāmaha

---

५. गतोऽस्तमको भातीन्दुर्यान्तिवासाय पक्षिणः ।
इत्येवमादि किं काव्यं वार्त्तामेनां प्रचक्षते ।।
—भामह, का० अ० २.८७

६. काव्य शोभा वहानां धर्माणां गुणव्यतिरिक्तत्वेसत्यलङ्कारत्वात् ।
-इन्दुराज, ल. वृ., पृ. १८

७. काव्य शोभायां: कर्त्तारोधर्मा गुणाः तदतिशय हेतवस्त्वलङ्काराः ।
—वामन, का० सू०, वृ० १.१.३

८. शब्दार्थौ सहितौ काव्यम् ।
—भामह, का० अ० १.१६

९. काव्यशब्दो यं गुणालङ्कार संस्कृतयोः शब्दार्थोयोवर्त्तते ।
—वामन १.१.१. पर वृत्ति

classified Alaṁkāra under two headings, based upon Śabda and Artha.[10] The wider application of this classification is available in Vāman's work. His division is bassed upon Śabda-Mūlaka and Upamā-Mūlaka.

Udbhaṭa does not mention the alaṁkāras under the heads of Śabdālaṁkāra and Arthālaṁkāra. More-over, the commentator of KASS. Rājānak Tilaka[1] states that this classification of alaṁkārs show the scanty knowledge of old rhetoricians. Udbhaṭa enumerates forty-one alaṁkāras under six varg*a*s and puts them according to their parity in each Varga. Besides few almost all alaṁkāras mentioned by Udbhaṭṭa fall part of the serialization of Bhāmaha. Indurāja is not at all careful to disclose the silent justification of alaṁkāras under six vargas which is descerned by Tilaka.

(B) ANALYTICAL STUDY OF ALAṀKĀRAS IN KASS WITH LAGHUVṚTTI

GROUP I

Udbhaṭa, the succesful follower of Bhāmaha, is avidly expanding his study on the treatment of figures into more lucid and scientific manner. He starts his work by surveying Bhāmaha and Daṇḍin and then systematically presents the definitions of 41 alaṃkāras with illustrations. He simply narrates these alaṃkāras without fixing the general characteristics of the word

---

१०. शब्दाभिधेयालङ्कारभेदादिष्टं द्वयं तु नः ।।

भामह, का० अ० १.१५

११. वर्गे वर्गेरलङ्कारापादानचिरन्तनालङ्काराक्ृतामल्पदर्शिता प्रकटयितुम् ।

—राजानक तिलक, ल० वि, पृ० १

'alaṃkāra'. The total alaṃkāras brought under an intelligible scheme with his original illustration quoted from his own Kumāra-Sambhava. When Kāvyacarchā was separated other developments took place and the Lakṣaṇa of Bharata transformed into some of the alaṃkāras afterwards. Bharata terms Lakṣaṇa as Kāvya Vibhūṣaṇa.[1] The number of alaṃkāras swell more and more from its previous stage in Bhāmaha's discussion of Kāvyālaṁkāra. The Ālaṁkārikas prefer to speak of one particular alaṁkāra in pre-Bhāmaha period.[21] In Sanskrit literature the style of works on poetics is of three types. Kārikā, sūtravṛtti and Kārikāvṛtti form and the flourishment of alaṃkāras in systematized presentation. He sustains its proficiency by the admixture of the naxus illustrations from his other work Kumāra-Sambhava.[3]

Udbhaṭa does not speak about the alaṁkāra 'yamaka'. In KASS. the शब्दाभ्यास of Bharata has been magnified into four figures of words, viz. Punarukta-Vadābhāsa, Chhekānuprāsa, Anuprāsa and Lāṭānuprāsa.[4] Yamaka of Bharata is only Śabdābhāsa,[5] which has been treated as Yamaka and Anuprāsa

---

१. एतानि काव्यस्य च लक्षणानि षट् त्रिंशदुद्देश्य निर्दर्शनानि ।
प्रबन्ध शोभाकराङ्गानि तज्जैः सम्यक् प्रयोज्या रसायमानि ।।
—भरत, नाट्यशास्त्र; १६.१७१

२. आनुप्रासिकं प्रचेता, यमकं यमः, चित्रं चित्राङ्गदः, शब्दश्लेषं शेषः, वास्तवं पुलस्त्यः, औपम्यमौपकायनः, अतिशयं पराशरः, अर्थ श्लेषमुतथ्यः, उभयालङ्कारिकं कुबेरः ।
—राजशेखरः, का० मी०, प्रथम अध्याय, पृ० १-२

३. अनेन ग्रन्थकृता स्वोपरचितकुमारसम्भवैकदेशोत्र उदाहरणत्वेनोपन्यस्तः ।
—इन्दुराज, ल. वृ., वर्ग १

४. पुनरुक्तवदाभासं छेकानुप्रास एव च ।
अनुप्रासस्त्रिधा लाटानुप्रासो रूपकं चतुः ।
—उद्भट, का० सा० सं०, वर्ग १, श्लोक १

by Bhāmaha and Vāmana. Rājaśekhara's Kāvya Mīmāṁsā state about the āchārya Yama who introduced Yamaka for the first time.[6] After Bharata another Āchārya Pracetāyana[7] says about 'Anuprāsa' independently for the first time because we have not found any hint of Anuprāsa in Bharata's time.[8] Anuprāsa procures the paramount importance till now in the filament of alaṃkāra literature. Udbhāṭa desists from Yamaka whereas Vāmana includes it into Śabdālaṃkāras.[9] Bhāmaha deals with Lāṭānuprāsa as a variety of Anuprāsa. The of Udbhaṭa is slightly illogical as he Latāṇuprāsa classifies into five varieties. Indurāja plans this alaṃkāra into five divisions on the basis of 'Svatantra' and 'Paratantra' order with accurate illustrations. In KASS. Udbhaṭa strives to stress on the elementaries of Punaruktavadābhāsa alaṃkāra as the first independent and innovatory one. At the beginning of his work KASS. he puts the name of Punarukta-vadābhāsa which is in neuter gender and also embellishes the poetry. Indurāja explains it as a बहुव्रीहि of five padas including two बहुव्रीहि of two padas each. Indurāja endeavours to the proposal of four

---

५. शब्दाभ्यासस्तु यमकमाभरत, नाट्यशास्त्र, १६.५६

६. यमकं यमः । — राजशेखर, का० मी०, अध्याय १, पृ० २

७. आनुप्रासिकं प्रचेतायनः । राजशेखर, का० मी०, पृ० २

८. उपमा रूपकं चैव दीपकं यमकं तथा ।
अलङ्कारास्तु विज्ञेयाश्चत्वारो नाटकाश्रयाः ।
—भरत, ना० शा०, १६.४०

९. पदमेनकार्थमक्षदंवा वृत्तं स्थाननियमे यमकम् ।
—वामन का० सू० वृ० ४.१.१

१०. लाटीयमप्यनुप्रासमिहेच्छन्त्य परे यथा
—भामह का० अ०, २.८

Śabdālaṁkāras[11] whereas Tilaka, another commentator of KASS. obtains Punarukta-vadābhāsa as the Ubhayālaṁkāra[12] and the rest three[12] into Śabdalāṃkāras.

The Chhekānuprāsa also originated by Udbhaṭa for the first time as a division of Bharata's Śabdābhyāsa. Though this seems to be an Anuprāsa, still it is not the division of Anuprāsa; rather it consists of the charming expression and collective pronunciation of similar vowels and consonants simultaneously.[14]

Indurāja, the commentator of KASS. diligently states that Bhāmaha has only two kinds of Anuprāsa and two kinds of Rupaka, whereas Udbhaṭa has three varieties of Anuprāsa and four of Rūpaka. This is also remarkably pointed out by Rājānaka Tilaka. According to Indurāja when Udbhaṭa says त्रिधा अनुप्रास it seems that 'धा' means (types) so it is of 3 types, but in चतुःरूपक, the termination is सुच् creates obstacles to comprehend the relation of चतुः with रूपक. This is why Indurāja clearly states with apt explanation.[15]

११. तत्र चादौ चत्वारः शब्दालङ्कारा निरूपिताः ।

—इन्दुराज, ल० वृ०, वर्ग १, पृ० १

१२. तत्राद्य उभयस्य शब्दस्यार्थस्य च ।

—राजानक तिलक, ल० वि०, वर्ग १, पृ० १

१३. तत त्रयः शब्दस्य ।

—राजानक तिलक, ल० वि०, वर्ग १, पृ० १

१४. छेकानुप्रासस्तु द्वयोर्द्वयोः सुसदृशोक्तिकृतौ ।

—उद्भट, का० सा० सं० १.३

१५. रूपकं चतुरित्यत्र रूपकत्वेन सहैकस्मिन्नर्थेवर्तमाना सत्ता रूपकभेदेष्वावर्तमाना प्रतीयते । अतः प्रतीयमाना यासौ रूपकत्वेकार्थसमवेता सत्तात्मिकाभवनक्रियातदभ्यावृत्तावयं—द्वित्रिचतुर्भ्यः सुच् इति सुत्प्रत्ययः, रूपकं चतुर्षु भेदेषु चतुरोवारान्भेदात्मना भवतीत्यर्थः ।

—इन्दुराज, ल० वृ०, पृ० २, वर्ग १

Anuprāsa occurs of three varieties, viz. Parūṣā, Upanāgarikā and Grāmyā. This fixture of Anuprāsa is to help the expression of sentiments.[16] Bhāmaha quotes the existence of Grāmyā mentioned by others in his Kāvyālaṃkāra. According to Udbhaṭa the composition of Anuprāsa seems to be of three kinds. Paruśā contains : श, ष, रेफ, टवर्ग whereas sparśa letters, Murdhanya letters are included in Upnāgarikā and Komalā (soft) letter लकार is meant to Grāmyānuprāsa. Indurāja also pays attention to this division.

The Kashmirian tradition represents Rūpaka as the prominent alaṃkāra. Bhāmaha puts it as a prevalent one. After discussing the two Śabdālaṃkāras he starts to touch the Rūpaka alaṃkāras.[17] Udbhaṭa also confesses about the latent importance of Rūpaka, as he belongs to the same Kashmirian school. He speaks about the (गौणीवृत्ति) Gauṇī Vṛtti in Rupaka[18] where the charm of Rūpaka is said to be of secondary significance. According to Daṇḍin, Rūpaka is treated as the तिरोभूत-

---

१६. एवमेतास्तिस्त्रावृत्तयो व्याख्याताः । तासु च रसाद्यभिव्यक्तयानुगुण्येन
पृथक् पृथगनुप्रासौ निबन्ध्यते ।

—इन्दुराज, ल० वृ०, पृ० ६, वर्ग १

१७. अनुप्रासः सयमको रूपकं दीपकीपमे ।
इतिवाचामलङ्कारा: प चैवान्येरुदाहृताः ॥

—भामह, का० अ०, २.४

१८. श्रुत्या सम्बन्धविस्तृतादय देन पदान्तरम् ।
गुणवृत्ति प्रधानेन युष्यते रूपकं तु तत् ॥

—उद्भट, का० सा० सं० १-११

भेदा[3] of Upamā and Bhāmaha[20] speaks about it as the existence of the common attributes, the identity of Upameya with Upamāna is called as Rūpaka. Udbhaṭa upholds the advancement of this definition of Bhāmaha. Indurāja adjudges this to into समस्तवस्तुविषय and एकदेशवर्त्तिरूपक which is similar Udbhaṭa.

Vāmana, a prolific āchārya of the Southern tradition has given much emphasis on Upamā-alaṃkāra which is predominent instead of Rūpaka of the औदीच्च school. The Southerns donot agree on the supremacy of Rūpaka. Bharata alludes Upamā in his Nāṭyaśāstra and supplies its wider application in Kāvya and its prime position in Poetics.[21] Vāmana extols Upama in his Upamā-prapañcha as the first and foremost alaṃkāra.[22] Vāmana classifies alaṃkāra into two divisions. Considering the importance of Upamā, he divides alaṃkāras in Śabdālaṃkāra and Upamāmūlaka alaṃkāra. Udbhaṭa defines Upamā as चेतोहारि साधर्म्यमुपमानोपमेययो[23] whereas Bhāmaha exhibits it as the साम्य of उपमान and उपमेय.[21]

---

१९. उपमेवतिरोभूतभेदा रूपक मुच्यते ।
—दण्डी, का० आ०, २.६६

२०. उपमानेन यत्तत्वमुपमेयस्य रूप्यते ।
गुणानां समतां दृष्ट्वा रूपकं नाम तद्विदुः ।।
—भामह, का० अ०, २.२१

२१. यत्किञ्चित् काव्यबन्धेषु सादृश्ये नोपमीयते ।
उपमा नाम सा ज्ञेया गुणाकृति समाश्रया ।।
—भरत, ना० शा० १६.४१

२२. उपमानेनोपमेयस्य गुणभेशतः साम्यमुपमा ।
—वामन, का० सू०, वृ० ४.२.१

२३. यच्चेतोहारि साधर्म्यमुपमानोपमेययोः ।
मियो विभिन्न कालादिशब्दयोरूपमा तु तत् ।
—उद्भट, का० सा० सं १.१५

२४. उपमेयस्य यत्साम्यं गुणलेशेन सोपमा ।
—भामह, का० अ०, २.३०

The commentator, Indurāja explains Upama and classifies it into seventeen categeries whereas Rājānak Tilaka divides it into twenty-one types.[25] Udbhaṭa considers four tattvas of Upamā, When these four tattvas Upameya, Upamāna, Sādharmya and Vācaka Śabda are represented, it is known as Ukta, while in the absence of tattvas one of these four, it is called anukta Upamā.

According to Udbhaṭa, Dīpaka is a significant alaṃkāra Bharata includes it as a prominent alaṃkāra.[26] Bhāmaha classifies Dīpaka into three divisions, viz. Ādi, Madhya and Anta.[27] It seems that Udbhaṭa also follows him in a way and differs from Vāmana. Bharata defines it as when different words illuminate among themselves remaining in one sentence it is called Dīpaka.[28] Bhāmaha has discussed the three types of Dīpaka simply avoiding its definition. Udbhaṭa, while following Bhāmaha, further adds two new viewpoints namely प्राधान्य and इतर and also includes into अन्तर्गतोपमा.[29] Indurāja agrees on

२५. तदेवमेषा सप्तदशविधा ग्रन्थकृता उपमा प्रतिपादिता ।

—इन्दुराज, ल० वृ० २१

२६. उपमा रूपकं चैवदीयकं यमकं तथा ।
अलङ्कारास्तु विज्ञेयाश्चत्वारी नाटकाश्रयाः ।।

—भरत, ना० शा०, २६.४०

२७. आदिमध्यान्तविषयं त्रिधा दीपकमिष्यते ।।

—भामह, का० आ०, २.२५

२८. नानाधिकरणस्थानां शब्दानां संप्रदीपतः ।
एक वाक्येन संयोगो यस्तद् दीपकमुच्यते ।।

—भरत, ना० शा० १६.५३

२९. आदिमध्यान्तविषयाः प्राधान्येतरयोगिनः ।
अन्तर्मतोपमाधर्मा यत्र तद्दीपकं विदुः ।।

—ऊद्भट, का० सा० सं० १.१४

this view of Udbhaṭa except speaking प्राधान्येतरयोगिनः[30] When he explains this alaṃkāra he also mentions the Kumāra Saṁbhava of Udbhaṭa. The Vivṛtikāra passes strictures upon the explanation of प्राधान्येतरयोगिनः given by Indurāja. He does not endorse that the sense of प्राधान्येतरयोगिनः is already expressed by अन्तर्गतोपमा and this प्राधान्य is only an अनुवाद by Indurāja. Dīpaka is not accepted by all the later writers, as some say that it is included under Tulya-Yogitā.

Here Indurāja arises one crusial question that Udbhaṭa in his Kārikā placed Dīpaka after Upamā but in stating the illustration he defines उपमा after दीपक and breaks out the order. Indurāja suggests that it should be firstly mentioned as Upamā, then Dīpaka would come later, according to the grammatical rule of यथोद्देशलक्षणम्. But to solve that problem Indurāja tells us that as Udbhata quotes some of the illustrations from Kumārasaṁbhava in his Kāvyālaṁkārasāra-saṁgraha. In order to maintain the metrical treatment, he did not mention Dīpaka before Upamā in his second kārikā of the first varga.[31]

Bhāmaha does not show the importance of Prativastūpamā he only mentioned it as an Arthālaṁkāra[32] and as a category

---

३०. एवं च प्राधान्येतरयोगिनः इत्ययमत्रानुवादः प्राप्तार्थत्वात् ॥

—इन्दुराज, ल० वृ० पृ० १५

३१. तत्र पूर्वं दीपकस्योदाहरणानि । तदनुसंधानाविछेदायात्र उद्देशक्रमः परित्यक्तः । उद्देश्यस्तु तथा न कृतो वृत्तभङ्गभयात् ॥

—इन्दुराज, ल० वृ०, वर्ग १

३२. समानवस्तु न्यासेन प्रतिवस्तूपमोच्यते ।
यथेवानभिधानेऽपि गुणसाम्यप्रतीतितः ॥

—भामह, का० अ०, २.३४

of Upamā, where the word यथा, इव is absent (क्रियासाम्यवाचकहीन) he calls it as the समासाभिहित उपमा.[33] Daṇḍin also mentions that this alaṃkāra is one variety of his Upamācakra.[34] According to Vāmana, the āchārya of southern tradition, the importance of Prativastūpamā shopes into a larger extent. He broadly divides it into शब्दमूलक and Upamāmūlaka.[35] Udbhaṭa speaks for the first time that Prativastūpamā is an independent alaṃkāra.[36] The Vivṛtikāra explains the Kārikā as his own view. He reads उपमावाचिशून्येयम् instead of उपमावाचिशून्यत्वम् and adds the comment that which belongs to the context is Upameya and the other is Upamāna. It remains without explanation in words and therefore should be seen later in somewhere else.

If, in general, appears to be the most satisfactory Varga of these alaṃkāras which describes about a well-organised group of alaṃkāra. Winding up the organization and explaination of this varga, we obtained an enhanced interest and consistent touch of Laghuvṛttikāra regarding the definition of Kāvya, general characteristics of 'Alaṃkāra' along with the independent identity of Śabdālaṃkāras and Arthālaṃkāras.

---

३३. विना यथेवशब्दाभ्यां समासाभिहितापरा ।

—भामह, का० अ० २.३२

३४. इयं प्रतीयमानैकधर्मावस्तूपमैव सा ।

—दण्डी, का० आ० २.१६

३५. उपमेयस्यौक्तौ समानवस्तुन्यासः प्रतिवस्तु ।

—वामन-का० सू० वृ० ४.३.२

३६. उपमानसंनिधाने च साम्यवाच्युच्यते बुधैर्यत्र ।
उपमेयस्य च कविभिः सा प्रतिवस्तूपमा गदिता ॥
प्राकरणिकेतरत्वस्थित्यैक श्चोपमेयतां लभते ।
उपमानत्वं चापरे इत्युपमावाचिशून्यत्वम् ॥

—उद्भट–का० सा० सं० १.२२-२३

This is a varga in which the Punaruktavadābhāsa, Chhekānuprāsa, Anuprāsa, Lāṭānuprāsa, Rūpaka, Dīpaka, Upamā and Prativastūpamā alaṃkāra are well-discussed with sub-divisions and accurate illustrations.

GROUP II

While discussing the second varga of KASS we reach on the conclusion that Udbhaṭa follows Bhāmaha in the division of this chapter. In fact, the entity of the beauty of these alaṃkāras are systematised and distinguished by Udbhaṭa. As soon as the excellent touch of the commentator it also seems enough clear with a baffled analysis.

Bhāmaha divides Ākṣepa of two types, viz. Vakṣamāṇa and Uktaviṣaya.[37] Daṇḍin states it as the Pratiṣedhokti.[38] Udbhaṭa gives much stress on the word 'Pratiṣedha iba'. He also illustrates the Ākṣepa by his own, though the origin of Ākṣepa is tracable from Bhāmaha.

'Viśeṣabhidhitsā' is the gist of this figure by Bhāmaha, but Daṇḍin refutes this and says Pratiṣedhokti (Real Nagation) is the Ākṣepa alaṃkāra. Vāmana also agrees on Daṇḍin's saying. Bhūta and bhaviṣya Ākśepa is stated by Bhāmaha. Vivṛttikāra speaks about Ākṣepa that the examples given by Udbhaṭa is useless. Indurāja comments directly and explains the nature of Ākṣepa and doesn't deviate from the Kārikā at all. To remove the difficulty which arise by प्रतिषेध

---

३७. वक्ष्यमाणोक्त विषयस्तत्राक्षेपो द्विधामतः ।
एकरूपतया शेषा निर्देक्ष्यन्ते यथाक्रमम् ॥

—भामह, का० अ०, २.६८

३८. प्रतिषेधोक्तिराक्षेपः ।

—दण्डी, का० अ० २.१२६

and इष्टमिव Indurāja introduces to emphasise the Kārikā निषेधनेव तइन्धी विधेयस्य चकोर्तित:. Here also he binds the division वक्ष्यमाणविषय and उक्तविषय would not be proper because the इष्ट (desired) may or may not be really expressed. So the negation refers to इष्ट it wouldn't be considered. Combining this Pratiṣedha and Vidheya Indurāja speaks of that when a thing desired to be asserted is actually expressed then the apparent negation of it is called Ākṣepa.[39]

We had observed that this alaṃkāra is more striking by the exposition at the hands of Indurāja. His discussion amounts to the elaborate show of the subordinate nature of Niṣedha. In Ākṣepa the Niṣedha does not obliterate the principal sense, on the contrary it heightens the greatness of the principal sense by the semblance of Pratisedha. So here he brings into the prominence of Vidheya Indurāja introduces Rudraṭa's definition and divisions of Ākṣepa[40] and applies the same to Udbhaṭa's examples and able to prove it.

The figure Arthāntaranyāsa is very meagrely connected with the Anumāna of Logicians, but Indurāja seems to indicate it is as real Anumāna having the Vyāpti and Pakshyadharmata in a veiled form. Arthāntarnyāsa requires Samarthyasamarthakabhāva[41] which is not the same as Karyakāranabhava or Vyāpyavyāpakabhāva that is required for the logical Anumāna. So infact it is the same as logical Anumāna and the poetical

---

३६. विधानकर्मता द्वारेणैवात्र इष्टत्वमवसीयते निबन्धनान्तराभावात् ॥

—इन्दुराज, ल० वृ०, वर्ग-२

४०. का० अ० रू०), ८.८६

४१. यत्र समर्थ्यसमर्थकभाव: सौर्थान्तरन्यास: । तत्र हि समर्थकस्य समर्थकतावशतिहेतुं व्यार्प्ति पक्षधर्मत्वं चानुपन्थस्यार्थान्तरस्यैवोपन्यास: क्रियते व्याप्ति पक्षधर्मत्वयो: स्वशव्देनानुपात्तयोरपि गर्भीकृतत्वात् ।

—लघुवृत्ति, प्रतीहारेन्दुराज:

charm. Udbhaṭa has not defined it, only he mentions it four divisions.[42] Bhāmaha speaks this alaṃkāra for the first time[43] and Vāmana also agrees on this point.

Udbhaṭa seems to have followed the definition of Bhāmaha regarding the Vyatireka alaṃkāra and he realises this alaṃkāra as a scientific and superior discussion which pertains to the art of poetic expression. The description of the superiority of Upamāna or Upameya is called as Vyatireka.[44] The idea of Bhāmaha is that where some superiority is stated with reference to Upameya the alaṃkāra is known as Vyatireka.[45] Udbhaṭa has improved Bhāmaha's definition of Vyatireka by introducing the expression निमित्तादृष्टिदृष्टिभ्यां and has brought two broad divisions of Vyatireka. Indurāja grasps the supreme importance of this alaṃkāra and its characteristics. And their he brings into two more divisions on account of the presence of absence of evādivācaka which has not touched by Udbhaṭa. By combining निमित्ता दृष्टिदृष्टिभ्यां द्विधा and यथोवादिसमन्वित: Indurāja manages to make the varieties four in number. He also remarks that विशेषापादनान्वय is the most important term

---

४२. समर्थकस्य पूर्वं यद्वचीन्यस च पृसृतः ।
विपर्ययेण वायत्स्याद्विशब्दोक्त्याऽन्यथापिवा ॥
ज्ञेयः सौर्थान्तरन्यासः —उद्भट, का० सा० सं० २.४

४३. उपन्यसनमन्यस्य यदर्थस्योदिताहते ।
ज्ञेयः सोऽर्थान्तरन्यासः पूर्वार्थानुगतो यथा ॥
—भामह, काव्यालङ्कारः, २.७१

४४. विशेषापादनं यत्स्यादुपमानोपमेययोः ।
निमित्तादृष्टिदृष्टिभ्यां व्यतिरेको द्विधा तु सः ॥
—उद्भट, का० सा० सं० २.६

४५. उपमानावतोऽर्थस्य यद्विशेष निदर्शनम् ।
व्यतिरेकं तमिच्छन्ति विशेषापादनापथा ॥
—भामह, का० अ०, २.७५

in Udbhaṭa's definition of Vyatireka. He has missed the real purport of the words Vaidharmeṇa Dṛṣṭanta Bhāmaha has no divisions of Vyatireka. Bhāmaha also does not include ādhikya of Upamāna over Upameya.[46]

Bhāmaha, Daṇḍin, Udbhaṭa, are not accepted Vibhāvanā as scientific principle. But the modern Rhetoricians treated it as a complementary the Visesokti and deal with it scienti ficailly. In the definition Udbhaṭa has used the word Kriyā[47] in the sense of Hetu. This has been used in the definition of Vibhāvanā by Bhāmaha,[48] Vāmana,[49] and Mammaṭa,[50] also. Udbhaṭa put the exact definition of Bhāmaha in case of Vibhāvanā Pratihārendurāja lucidly and simply agrees on this and comment this idea of Udbhaṭa as the same expression with the example अङ्गलेखामकाश्मीरसमा etc.

Udbhaṭa's definition of Samāsokti[51] figure is more com-

---

४६. उपमानबतोर्थस्य यद्विशेष निदर्शनम् ।
व्यतिरेकं तमिच्छन्ति विशेषापादनाद्यथा ॥
—भामह, का० अ०, २.७५

४७. क्रियायाः प्रतिषेधे या तत्फलस्य बिभावना ।
—उद्भट, का० सा० सं० २.६

४८. क्रियायाः प्रतिषेधे या तत्फलस्य विभावना ॥
—भामह, का० अ०, २.७७

४९. क्रियायाः प्रतिषेधो प्रसिद्धतत्फलव्यक्तिर्विभावना ।
—वामन, का० सू० वृ० ३.२

५०. क्रियायाः प्रतिषेधेपि फलव्यक्तिर्विभावना ।
—मम्मट, का० प्र० —१०

५१. प्रकृतार्थेन वाक्येन तत्समानैर्विशेषणैः ।
अप्रस्तुतार्थकथनं समासोक्तिरुदाहृता ॥
—उद्भट, का० सा० सं० २.१

plete, scientific than that of Bhāmaha.[52] He has advanced greatly with exactness and accuracy. Bhāmaha and Dandin are not at all aware as to whether the अभिप्रेतार्थ should be अप्रकृत and उक्तार्थ to be अप्रकृत and vice verse. But अभिप्रेतार्थ प्रकृत and उक्तार्थ अप्रकृत is already given by Udbhaṭa.

The concept of Indurāja's commentary was born as a supplement to make more strengthen and developed to Udbhaṭa's ideas on Alaṃkāras. Though Atiśayokti alaṃkāra has got broader aspects viz. वक्रोक्ति[53] (Vakrokti) recognises this and it counted as the origin of Kāvya and सौन्दर्य,[54] गुणातिशय by Bhāmaha still he didn't divide[55] into any categories. Udbhaṭa for the first time makes it into four division.[56] Udbhaṭa's definitions[57] is similar to Bhāmaha in defining this alaṃkāra.

---

५२. यत्तोक्ते गम्यतेऽन्योऽर्थस्तत्समानविशेषरणः ।
सा समासोक्तिरुद्दिष्टा संक्षिप्तार्थतया यथा ।।
—भामह, का० अ०, २.७९

५३. सैषा सर्वेव वक्रोक्तिरनयार्थो विभाव्यते ।
यत्नोऽस्यां कविना कार्यः कोऽलंकारोऽनयाविना ।।
—भामह. का० अ०, २.८४

५४. इत्येवमादिरुदिता गुणातियर्थागतः ।
सर्वेवातिशयोक्तिस्तु तर्कचेत्तां यथागमम् ।।
—भामह, का० अ०, २.८५

५५. निमित्ततो वयो यत्तु लोकातिक्रान्तगोचरम् ।
मन्यन्तेऽतिशयोक्ति ताभल[illegible] रतया यथा ।।
—भामह-का० अ०, २.८१

५६. भेदेनन्यत्वमन्यत्त नानात्वं यत्र बध्यते ।
तथा संभाव्यमानार्थनिवन्धेतिशयोवितगीः ।।
कार्यकारणयोर्यत्र पौर्वापर्यविपर्ययात् ।
आशुभावं समालम्व्य बध्यते सोऽपि पूर्ववत् ।।
—उद्भट, का० सा० सं० २.१२-१३

Udbhaṭa gives much stress on the word लोकातिक्रान्तगोचरम् which he has directly borrowed from Bhāmaha.

Udbhaṭa has not only attempted classification but has succeeded a great deal in making distinct divisions of the figure, which is taken by the later authors as the base of treatment.

Thus, the second varga of Udbhaṭa developed clearly by the ably observation of Indurāja.[57]

GROUP III

This coming instalment is consisted three alaṃkāras in the same order of Bhāmaha where Udbhaṭa analyses the Yathāsaṁkhya, Utprekṣā and Svabhāvokti. This is also more clear by the trend of thought of Indurāja. The brilliant stress on the word 'असधर्मत्व'[58] in Yathāsaṁkhya alaṁkāra has paid by Bhāmaha, which has not been accepted by Daṇḍin. As Bhāmaha refers that Medhāvin says it as the figure 'Saṃkhyāna'.[59] Daṇḍin gives three names to this figure, viz. Yathā-

---

५७. निमित्ततो यत्तु वचो लोकातिक्रान्तगोचरम् ।
मन्यन्तेतिशयोक्ति तामलंकारतया बुधाः ॥

—उद्भट-का० सा० सं० २.११

Compare with Bhāmaha, 2.81

५८. भूयसामुपदिष्टानामर्थानामसधर्मणाम् ।
क्रमशो योऽनुनिर्देशो यथासंख्यं तदुच्यते ॥

—भामह-का० अ०, २.८९

५९. यथासंख्यमथोत्प्रेक्षामलङ्कारद्वयं विदुः ।
संख्यानमिति मेधाविनोत्प्रेक्षाभिहिता क्वचित् ।

—भामह, का० अ०, २.८८

saṃkhya, Saṁkhyāna and Krama.[60] Udbhaṭa agrees on Bhāmaha so quotes half of this from him.[61] But Indurāja points out that असधर्मणाम् and establishes his own view bringing the example of Rudraṭa.[62] He suggests that if there be similarity between the two groups, then the alaṃkāra will always by Vyatireka, Upamā, Rūpaka and the element of Yatrāsaṁkhya will be thrown into the back ground. So he shows the मृणाल, हंस, पद्म should have dissimilar with बाहु, चङ्क्रमण and आनन.[63] Otherwise it will become the example of Vyatireka. He comprehends that the groups of objects should be असधर्म which expatiates upon the properity of the expression असधर्मणाम् in the definition.

The next important figure which had found a place in Bhāmaha's Kāvyālaṃkāra is known as Utprekśā.[64] Udbhaṭa borrows his last line from Bhāmaha.[65] Daṇḍin tries to empha-

---

६०. यथासंख्यमिति प्रोक्तं संख्यानंक्रमइत्यपि ।
—दण्डी०, का० द०, २.२७३

६१. भूयसामुपदिष्टा नामर्थानामसधर्मणाम ।
क्रमशो योनुनिर्देशे यथासंख्यं तदुच्यते ।।
—उद्भट का० सा० सं० ३.२., पृ० ४५

६२. कज्जलहिमकनक सदः सुपर्णवृषकं सवाहनाः शंवः ।
जलनिधिगिरि पद्मस्था हरिहरचतुरानना ददतु ।।
—का० अ० (रू०) ७.३६

६३. पद्मेन्दुभृङ्ग मानङ्ग पुष्कोकिल कलापिनः ।
—भामह, का० अ०, २.६०

६४. अतद्गुणक्रियायोगादुत्प्रेक्षातिशयान्विता ।
—भामह, का० अ०, २.६१

६५. साम्यरूपाविवक्षायां वाच्येवाद्यात्मभिः पदैः ।
अतद्गुणक्रियायोगादुत्प्रेक्षातिशयान्विता ।।
—उद्भट, का० सा० सं० ३.३

sise this by dividing into चेतनगत and अवचेतनगत.[66] Udbhaṭa also influences on Daṇḍin and describes it as लोकातिकान्त विषया.[67] To strengthen this idea of Udbhaṭa, Indurāja brings an example which does not contain इवादिशब्द. Udbhaṭa also adds stress on the word अतद्‌गुणसंभावना like Bhāmaha and this अतद्गुणसंभावना is for the sake of अतिशय.

For the first time we caught sight of Svabhāvokti in the work of Bhāmaha which shows the exactness of 'Vastu-svabhāva'[68] is merely recognised as an alaṃkāra. By stating 'इति केचित्प्रचक्षते' it seems that Bhāmaha didnot accept it as alaṃkāra, rather it is as the basis[69] of Kāvya. Daṇḍin classifies Svabhāvokti into four kinds i.e. Jāti, Kriyā, guṇa and dravya.[70] In the province of Śāstra[71] the role of 'Svābhāvika'

---

६६. अन्यथैव स्थिता वृत्ति श्चेतमस्येतरस्यवा ।
अन्यथोत्प्रेक्ष्यते यत्र तामुत्प्रेक्षां विदुर्यथा ॥
—दण्डी, का आ० २.२२१

६७. लोकातिक्रान्तविषया भावाभावाभिमानतः संभावनेयमुत्प्रेक्षा ।
—उद्भट, का० सा० सं० पृ० ४७

इयं चीत्प्रक्षाबहिः असंभवत पदार्थस्य सभवद्रूपतयीपवर्णानात्मीका तिक्रान्तविषया संभावना ॥
उद्‌भट, का० सा० सं० पृ० ४७ पर ल. वृ.

६८ स्वभावोक्तिरलङ्कार इति केचित्प्रचक्षते ।
अर्थस्य तदवस्थात्वं स्वभावो भिहितो यथा ॥
—भामह, का० अ०, २.९३

६९. युक्तं वक्रस्वभावौक्त्या सर्वमेवादिष्यते ।।
—भामह, का० अ०, १.३०

७०. जाति क्रिया गुण द्रव्यवाचिनेक त्रवर्त्तिना ।
सर्ववाक्योपचार श्चोत्तदाहुर्दीपकं यथा ॥
—दण्डी, का० आ०, २.९७

७१. शास्त्रे स्वयस्यैव साम्राज्यं काव्येष्वण्येत दीप्सितम् ।
—दण्डी, का० आ०, २.१३

is very significant as well as its importance in Kāvya is not ignorable, so Daṇḍin admits it as the best[72] alaṃkara.

Daṇḍin also calls this as Svabhāvokti, Jāti and Svabhāvākhyāna.[73]

Udbhaṭa cites the significance of the Kriyā for the factual description of 'Chetan' Padārtha' (living substance). This is the novelty of Udbhaṭṭa which carries the unwarranted restriction of the scope of Svabhāvokti to the 'Hevāka',[74] eagerness in their respective activities of young ones of animals and the like. Rājānak Tilak[75] explains it as a description of the nature of things as such is not svabhāvokti but only the 'Hevāka' of Bālamṛga and the same in their activities.[76] But Indurāja liberally interprets Hevāka and enlarges the scope of this figure to its normaley.[77]

The conclusion is that the idea represented by this varga concerning the improvement of alaṃkaras and its illustrations

---

७२. वाचामुत्तमभूषणं..................।

—दण्डी, का. ग्रा.

७३. स्वभावोक्ति उपजातिश्चेत्थाद्यासालंकृतिर्यथा ॥

—दण्डी, का० ग्रा० २.८

७४. क्रियायां संप्रवृत्तस्य हेवाकानां निबन्धनम् ।
कस्यचिन्मृगांडम्मोदः स्वभावोक्तिरुदाहृता ॥

—उद्भट, का० सा० सं०, ३.५, पृ० ४६

७५. व्यापार प्रवृत्तस्य वालमृगादेः समुचित हेवाक
निबन्धनं स्वभावोक्तिः । न तु स्वभावमात्र कथनम् ॥

—राजानक तिलक, ल० वि०, वर्ग ३

७६. मृगबालादेः स्वसमुचिते व्यापारे प्रवृत्तस्य ये हेवाकाः स्वजात्यानुरूप्येणाभिनिवेशविशेषास्तदुपनिबन्धः स्वभावोक्तिः ।

—इन्दुराज, ल० वृ०, वर्ग ३, पृ० ४६

७७. ग्रद्य या मम गोविन्त जाता त्वयि गृहागते ।
काले नैषा भवेत्प्रीतिस्तवैवागमनात्पुनः ॥

—भामह, का० ग्र०, ३.५

is substantially ennobling and noteworthy. In case of Svabhāvokti, the author cites the significance of Kriyā which is also agreed by Indurāja.

GROUP IV

Udbhaṭa has something special to contribute to the study of his fourth chapter. He has touched this chapter by acute appreciation with the connection of rasa, bhāva, āvāsa, praśama. Bhāmaha's treatment of Preya alaṃkāra only stating the example without giving the definition which is very much similar to Mahābhārata. By applying the termination Udbhaṭa says it as (प्रेयस्वत् अलंकार) Preyasvat figure. Daṇḍin, Ruyyako, Mammaṭa also use the word Preyas. In preyasvat Udbhaṭa is concerned with Sthāyībhāva. The definition of रत्यादिकानां भावानाम् and Vivṛtikāra Tilaka adds रतियिहेदेवगुरू नृपाधिविषया गृह्यते, कान्ता विषमायाः स्तुतेः सूपठो रसवदलंकारो वक्ष्यते. Indurāja says 'रतिश्रययूनोर्मन्मथात्मिका' which supplies more authenticity to Udbhaṭa's definition about रति in Preyasvat. Daṇḍin's प्रेयस् is प्रेयतराख्यानम्.[78]

Udbhaṭa recognises rasas and bhāvas but relegates them to a subordinate position by including them all in the alaṃkāras. Rasavat, Preyasvata, Ūrjasyi, Samāhita alaṃkāras, In the definition of Rasavat the nine rasas[79] are coun ted

---

७८. प्रेयः प्रियत्तराख्यानं ।

—दण्डी, का० आ० २.२७५

७९. शृङ्गारहास्यकरूण रौद्रवीरभयानकाः ।
वीभत्साद्भुत शान्ता नव नाट्ये रसाः स्मृताः ॥

—उद्भट, का० सा० सं० ४.४

This Kārikā has been quoted from ना० शा० of भरत

Cont......

by Udbhaṭa which is also admitted by Indurāja. It seems that during his time, Śānta rasa was also developed as the ninth rasa in the Sanskrit literature. By saying rasa, Udbhaṭa also able to show the स्वशब्द, स्थायी, संचारी, विभाव, and अभिनय.[80] Here Indurāja does not pay more attention to discuss the wider exposition of rasa and bhāva which is not discriminated. So he wants a plea to escape, this needless context and stops its swelling volumes.[81]

According to Udbhaṭa, the sketch of rasa, together with its constituents, produces the figure Rasavat, the delineation of Sthāyīs like Rati etc. produces the figure preyasvat. By the delightful nature of Rasavat alaṃkāra the पुरुषार्थ चतुष्टय[82] is obtained. Udbhaṭa[83] borrows the idea from Bhāmaha and he

---

by Udbhaṭa. It is also found in Udbhaṭa's gloss on Nāṭyaśāstra which is not available. There are 8 rasas are counted but later on Śānta was accepted as the 9th rasa in Nāṭyaśāstra. Some of the poeticians say that this rasa is concerned only with Kāvya not with the Nāṭya. Anyhow, Udbhaṭa refers nine rasas in this Kārikā of KASS.

८३. स्वशव्द स्थायिसंचारिविभावामिनयास्पदम् ।

—उद्‌भट, का० सा० सं० ४ ३

८१. रसानां भावानां च काव्यशोभातिशयहेतुत्वात् किं काव्यालङ्कारप्वमुत काव्यजीवितत्वमिति न तावद्विचार्यते ग्रन्थ गौरवीभयात् । रसाभावस्वरूपं चात्र न विवेचितम् प्रकृतावाद्वहुवक्तव्यत्वाच्च ।

—इन्दुराज, ल० वृ०, वर्ग-४

८२. चतुर्वर्गेतरौ प्राप्य परिहार्यौं क्रमाद्यतः ।
चैतन्यभेदादास्वाद्यात्स रसस्ताद्दशोमतः ।।

—इन्दुराज, ल० वृ०, वर्ग ४

८३. रसवद्यदर्शितस्पष्टश्रृङ्गारादि रसादियम् । भामह, काव्यालङ्कार ३.६
स्वशव्द स्थायिसंचारि विभावाभिनयास्पदम् ।

—उद्भट, का० सा० सं० ४.३

expresses it more accurate and clear. Indurāja celebrates the meaning of 'rasa' and declares that when the general relishment is sought to be expressed, the rasa may be used for निर्वेद, ग्लानि, as in the case of मधुर, अम्ल. This is available in Rudraṭa's Kārikā[84] conveying the same meaning. The sentiments are the means of achieving four fold objects and avoiding their opposite which are known as nine Sthāyibhāvas in an appreciated manner.

In case of the figure Ūrjasvi, Bhāmaha has not left any definition.[85] Udbhaṭa says that Ūrjasvi has related with rasābhāsa and bhāvābhāsa, Daṇḍin has also not defined Urjasvi. According to Udbhaṭa the improper elements of bhāva and rasa is called Ūrjasvi. Indurāja, also reaches on this point regarding this figure. The improper delineation of rasa and bhāva provide the existence of this which is known as Rasābhāsa and Bhāvābhāsa.

We can see the illustration of Samāhita, without the definition in Bhāmaha's work. This is called samāhita by Udbhaṭa and the laters called it as Samādhi-Alaṃkāra. Indurāja also admits to Udbhaṭa and brings a more clear concept on this figure, He says that the convention of Śāstra are explained by the consistent of rasa and bhāvas.[86] The

---

८४. रसनादसत्वमेषां मधुरादीनामिवोक्तमाचार्यैः ।
निर्वेदादिष्वपि तत्प्रकाममस्तीति तेपि रसाः ॥

—का० अ० (रू०) १२.४

८५. ऊर्जस्वि कर्णेन यथा पार्थाय पुनरागतः ।
द्वि सन्दधाति किं कर्णः शलये त्यहिरपाकृतः ।

—भामह, का० अ०, ३.७

८६. इह रसभावानां शास्त्रसमयाविरुद्धेन तद्धि रूद्धेन च रूपेण द्वै विध्यमुक्तम् ।

—इन्दुराज, ल० वृ० अध्याय-४, पृ० ५६

inconsist elements are known as रसाभास and भावाभास. When it will completely vanish the operating sentiments and feelings are called as Samāhita. By the cessation of old sentiment, the new one being introduced, and established as rasavat and others. While the delineation of the rasa (प्रशम), bhāva etc. constitutes and the cessation of total void of the Anubhāvas is called as figure Samāhita by Udbhaṭa.[87] Indurāja also admits this subdueing of sentiments in Samāhita alaṃkāra.

Udbhaṭa tries to define completely and clearly Bhāmaha's[88] definition of पर्यायोक्त so he borrows the exact sentence from him and by adding own knowledge he establishes पर्यायोक्त अलंकार.[89] When we come to this alaṃkāra of Udbhaṭa we find an accurate mention of a significant capacity called अवगम,[90] which means 'suggestion'. It means a capacity different from and coming after the abhidhā of the words and tātparya of the sentence as a whole, Indurāja has an ambition to explain the वाचकवृत्ति and वाच्यवृत्ति by viewing his own words.[91] Indurāja also says

---

८७. रसभावतदाभासवृत्तैः प्रशमबन्धनम् ।
अन्यानुभावनिः शून्यरूपं यत्तत्समाहितम् ।।
—उद्भट, का॰ सा॰ सं॰ ४.७ पृ॰ ५६

८८. पयर्यायोक्तं यदन्येन प्रकारेणाभिधीयते ।
उवाच रत्नाहरणे चैद्यं शार्ङ्गधनुर्यथा ।।
—भामह, का॰ अ॰, ३.८

८९. पर्यायोक्तं यदन्येन प्रकारेणाभिर्धीयते ।
वाच्यवाचकवृत्तिभ्यां शून्येनावगमात्मना ।।
--उद्भट, का॰ सा॰ सं॰ ४.६, वर्ग-४

९०. वाच्यवाचकवृत्तिभ्यां शून्येनावगमात्मना ।
—उद्भट-का॰ सा॰ सं॰ ४.६

९१. वाचकस्या भिधायकस्य स्वशव्दस्य वृत्तिर्व्यापारो वाच्यार्थं प्रत्यायनम् ।
—इन्दुराज, ल॰ वृ॰ पृ॰ ५५

that the वस्तुध्वनि is included in पर्यायोक्त अलंकार.[92]

Udbhaṭa firstly present the advanced description of Udātta and it became the definite source of the successive achāryas. He terms Udātta as the propoundation of prosperity of wealth and characteristic of the great personality[93] Udātta is also called as Udāra by Bhaṭṭi and Aasara by Rudraṭa. Udbhaṭa also admits the idea of Daṇḍin[94] in this alaṃkāra. Udbhaṭa tries to show it as an independent identity so by adding उपलक्षणतां with महात्मचरित he speaks the plenty wealth or the deeds of noble character as a secondary sense. By this sense this differs from Rasavat. Thus Indurāja also appears on this description of the figure Udātta by his author.

Regarding Śliṣṭa we have found that Udbhata clearly defines about the overall importance of Ślista for the first time. According to him Śliṣṭa is of two types; Śabdaśliṣṭa and Arthā-śliṣṭa[95]. But Daṇḍin classifies it into अभिन्नपद and भिन्नपद.[96] The

---

९२. अतोत्र वस्तुमात्रस्यैवंविधस्य शब्दव्यापारास्पृष्टस्य प्रमीयमा नता । तद्विषयस्य चकाव्यधर्मस्य ध्वनमाभिधानस्य वाच्यवाचक व्यापार-शून्यावगमनस्वभावत्वात्पर्यायोक्तालङ्कार संसर्पशित्वम् ।

—इन्दुराज, ल० वृ०, पृ० ८६

९३. उदात्तमृधिमहूस्तु चरितं च महात्मनाम् ।
उपलक्षणतां प्राप्तं नेतिवृत्तत्वमागतम् ।।

—उद्भट, का० सा० सं० ४-८

९४. आशयस्य विभूतेर्वा यन्महत्वनुत्तमम् ।
उद्रात्तं नाम तं प्राहुरलङ्कारं मनीषिणः ।।

—दण्डी, का० आ० २ ३००

९५. द्वि विधैटार्थशब्दोक्तिविशिष्टं तत्प्रतीयताम् ।

—उद्भट—का० आ० सं०, ४.१०

९६. श्लिष्टमिष्टमनेकार्थमेकरूपान्वितं वचः ।
तदभिन्नपदं भिन्नपदप्रायमितिद्विधा ।।

—दण्डी, का० आ० २.३१०

modern writers have changed the title of श्लिष्ट into śleṣa. And also a great Change has seen in between Udbhaṭa and modern rhetoricians śleṣa division. The figure Śleṣṭa's province is governed by other alaṃkāras and Indurāja says that other alaṃkāras reced and give prominence to Śliṣṭa, otherwise it will be thrown and entirely lost its background[97]. But Mammaṭa refutes the principle of एप्रकयत्नोच्चार्यता of (Indurāja) also agrees on two varieties of Śleṣa)[99] Udbhaṭa. Indurāja explains the Śliṣṭa becomes an alaṃkāra by creating an image of other alaṃkāras.[100] It has no independent existence.[101] Indurāja elucidātes the peculiarity's of Udbhaṭa.[102] Śleṣa is of two types.

शब्द and अर्थ and both are अर्थालंकार by Udbhaṭa but it vehemently criticises by Mammaṭa.[103] Śleṣa is thc principal figure so that apprehension of the others is dispelled by it saying by Udbhaṭa.[104]

---

९७. अतोनेनाववकाशत्वात्स्वाविषये अलङ्कारान्तराण्यपोद्यन्ते तेषां विषयान्तरे सावकाशत्वात् ।

—इन्दुराज, लघुवृत्ति, वर्ग ४

९९. तदेवं शब्दश्लिष्टमर्थश्लिष्टं च लक्षितम् ।

—इन्दुराज, ल० वृ०, वर्ग-४

१००. अलङ्कारान्तरगतां प्रतिमां जनयत्पदैः ।

—इन्दुराज, ल० वृ०, वर्ग-४

१०१. अतोमेनानवकाशत्वात्स्वाविषये अलङ्कारान्तराज्यपोद्यरे तेषां विषयान्तरे सावकाशत्वात् ।

—इन्दुराज, मधुवृत्ति, वर्ग-४

१०२. अर्थभेदेन तावच्छब्दा शिद्यन्त इति भट्टद्भिटक्ष्य सिद्धान्त ।

—इन्दुराज, ल० वृ०

१०३. शब्दश्लेष इति चोच्यते, अर्थालङ्कारमध्ये च गाक्ष्यते इति कोयं नयः ।

—मम्मट, का० प्र०, बिलास-९, पृ० २१५

१०४. अलङ्कारान्तरगतां प्रतिभां जनयत्पदैः ॥

—उद्भट-का० सा०, सं०, ४-१०

Now it is important to remember that the allusions to a similar association three figures like Preyasvat, Rasavat, Uujasvi, Samāhita, Paryāyokta, Udātta and Śliṣṭa stand a splendours position.

In the context of Nātya the ninth rasa discussion is also an important achievement must have enjoyed highest supposition.

GROUP—V

Udbhaṭa's definition of Apahnuti[105] is practically as same as that of Bhāmaha.[106] Daṇḍin[107] has quite different definition of this figure. He does not seem to hold that उपमानोपमेयभाव as to from Apahnuti. Indurāja admits the उपमेयानोपमेयभाव.[108]

The varieties of Viśeṣokti is analysed by Udbhaṭa with a new definition. He polishes Bhāmaha's Viśeṣokti[109] and of to some extent he omits Bhāmaha and proves his own acceptance

---

१०५. अपह्नुतिरभीस्टा च किंचिदन्तर्गतोपमा ।
भूतार्थापह्नवादस्था: क्रियते चाभिधा यथा ।।

—भामह, का० अ०, ३.२१

१०६. अपह्नुतिरभीष्टा च किंचिदन्तर्गतोपमा ।
भृतार्थापहनवेमास्या: निबन्ध: क्रियते बुधै: ।।

—उद्भट, का. सा. सं. पृ० ५३

१०७. अपह्नुनिरपह्नुत्य किंचिदन्यार्थदर्शनम् ।
मप चेषु: स्मरतस्य सहस्रं पात्रिणामिति ।।

—दण्डी, का० आ. २.३०४

१०८. यत्र भूतं विद्यमानमुपमेय लक्षणमर्थपहनुत्योपमान
रूपारोपणोपमानोपमेयभावो (—वगम्यते सोपहनु-) तिरलङ्कार: ।

—इन्दुराज, ल० वृ०, वर्ग-५

१०९. एकदेशस्य विगमे या गुणान्तरसंस्थित: ।
विशेषप्रथनायासौ विशेषोक्तिर्मता यथा ।।

— भामह, का. अ. ३.०३

(idea). Bhāmaha doesn't require the presence of कार्यकारणभाव and the non-occurence of Result or Kārya as the important elements of the figure.[110] Indurāja admits Udbhaṭa's definition and classifies it into two types. The फलानुपावृत्ति and निमित्तादर्शन and some times it is also observed as the लक्ष्य and लक्षण style.

"The expression of a thing different and contradictory to the quality or action of the dravya वस्तु) for the purpose of establishing the excellence (of it) is called Virodha."[111]

The definition of Virodha given by Udbhaṭa seems incomplete so Indurāja supplies द्रव्य (गुणस्य वा क्रियाया ला...).[3] The Vivṛtikāra adds जाति and द्रव्य. Indurāja's discussion calculates to this विरुद्धा या अन्या क्रिया.

"The expression conveying similarity between things that are both अप्रस्तुत or between things that are both प्रस्तुत, the things themselve not being intended either as उपमात or उपमेय, is तुल्ययोगिता.[112]

In तुल्ययोगिता Udbhaṭa has approached towards Mammaṭa and has left aside Bhāmaha and Daṇḍin. Udbhaṭa shows the difference between Dīpaka and Tulyayogitā by saying there is no उपमातोपमेयभाव and both or all the parties are either प्रस्तुत or अप्रस्तुत in Tulyayogttā.

The fifth varga involved a deep concern for the establishment of alaṃkāras. With the means of supporting alaṃkāra, the role of अप्रस्तुतप्रशंसा, संकठ is ripened to maturity and keeping a firm hold over the alaṃkāra literature.

"The commendatory statement of an object removed from the principal them of description but conveying with it a sense of the principal theme (प्रस्तुत), is called अप्रस्तुतप्रशंसा.[113]

११०. यत्सामग्र्येपि शक्तीनां फलानुत्पत्तिबन्धनम् ।
विशेषस्याभिधित्सातस्तद्विशेषोक्तिरुच्यते। ।

—उद्भट, का. सा. ५.४, पृ७ ६२

१११. KASS with Laghuvṛtti, N.D. Banhatti, p. 123.

११२. KASS with Laghuvṛtti, N,D. Banahqtti, p. 125.

११३. KASS with Laghuvṛtti, N.D. Banhatti, p, 127

Udbhaṭa has improved अप्रस्तुतप्रशंसा alaṃkāra by putting प्रस्तुतार्थानुबन्धिनी. Daṇḍin has a very different type of अप्रस्तुतप्रशंसा. The प्रस्तुतार्थानुबन्धिनो achieves a great amount of success otherwise according to Indurāja it will be considered as the raings of a mad man.[114]

Where censure is meant by the (direct) potentiality of words, but where praise is really desired to be principally understood the figure is व्याजस्तुति.[115]

Udbhaṭa seems to admit only व्यार्जेनस्तुतिः व्याजस्तुतिः. He also recognising where निन्दा is apparent and स्तुति is real and forms the example likely.[116]

When he impossible relation between two things or a possible one causes comparison (उवमानोपमेयभाव) between the two things to be understood, then the figure is called विदर्शना[117]

Indurāja explains the word विदर्शना according to its etymological sense. Now the word विदर्शना is very uncommon and not used. All the writters except Udbhaṭa have uniformly used the word निदर्शना and nobody even tries to hint the varient विदर्शना as used somewhere. Indurāja also invariably writes विदर्शनो deriving the word with the 'वि' उपसर्ग by the expression 'विशिष्टयार्थस्य'. But the vivṛtikāra speaks it as निदर्शना as the Madras Ms. also contains निदर्शना on the basis of भवन्वस्तु सम्बन्ध and अभवन्व-

११४. न चैवमपि तस्या उन्मत्तप्रलापप्रख्याततायतः सा केनचित्स्वाजन्येन प्रस्तुतमर्थमनुबन्धाति तदुक्तम् प्रस्तुतार्थानुबन्धिनी इति ।

—इन्दुराज, ल० वृ०, वर्ग-५

११५. N.D. Banhatti, p. 129.

११६. धिगनन्योपमामेतां तावकां रूपसंपदम् ।
त्रैलोक्येप्यनुरूपो यद्वरस्तव न लभ्यते ॥

—उद्भट, का० सा० सं., ५.८

११७. KASS with Laghuvṛtti, N.D. Banhatti, p. 130

सम्बन्ध[118]. Indurāja[419] says that though Udbhaṭa mentions the उपमानोपमेयत्वं still he has not given the illustration of this उपमानोपमेयत्वं of विदर्शना[120]. So Indurāja brings illustration from Bhāmaha's Kāvāylaṃkāra for this उपमानोपमेयभाव of विदर्शना.

Saṁkara is the admixture of two figures. It is not an alaṃkāra by itself. Bhāmaha has no Saṃkara alaṃkāra only he has treated to Saṃsṛṣṭi as an alaṃkāra. Bhāmaha told the combination of Upamā-rūpaka and Utprekṣāvayava as Saṃṣṛṭi whereas Vāmana speaks these along with Saṅkara alaṃkāra. But Udbhaṭa believes it as an independent alaṃkāra and he differentiates Saṅkara from Saṃsṛsi. Udbhaṭa categories Saṃkara into four types : Sandeha Saṁkara. Śabdārthvatya alaṃkāra Saṁkara Ekaśabdābhidhāna Saṁkara and Aṅgāṅgi-bhāva Saṁkara.

The opinion of Indurāja putforth the quite clear explanation in these four classification of Saṁkara. Before Udbhaṭa the ideas of Daṇḍin and Bhāmaha are not elaborate and systematic. So Indurāja takes the systematic definitions of this figure and describes its advancement which helps to establish its recognition in Alaṁkāra literature.

"When comparison is reciprocal, the object being to remove the possiblity of all other comparisons, (the figure) is

११८. अभवनस्तु संबन्धी भवन्ना यत्र कल्पयेत् ।
उपमानोपमेयत्वं कथ्यते सा विदर्शना ॥
—उद्भट, का० भा० सं०, ५.१०

११९. यत्र तु पदार्थसमन्वय उपमानोपमेयभावकल्पनया स्वात्मानमुपपादयति तस्य निदर्शनाभेदस्योदस्योदाहरणमुद्भतपुस्तके न दृश्यते । तस्य तु भामीहीदिति मिदमुदाहरणम् ।
—इन्दुराज, ल० वृ०, वर्ग-५

१२०. अयं मन्दद्युतिर्भास्वामस्तं प्रतियियासति ।
उदय: पतनायेति श्रीमतीबोधचकारान् ॥
—भामह, का० अ०, ३.३४

called Upameyapamā"[121] Upameya is that which being a thing to the comparison is Prākaraṇika. In the verse शिरांशिपङ्कजानीव etc. the Kara and Cakra are both Prākaraṇika for the prowess of Viṣṇu's 'Kara' and Cakra and both are Upameyas. Indurāja clearly states the word पक्षान्तरहानिगाम् to avoid the doubt on Prākaraṇikatva.

Indurāja says the example of Dīpaka would come under Sahokti the two actions must be happen simultaneously, depending upon two different things are described by one word. To eradicate the doubt in the example संजहाररंत्काल etc. which falls under Dīpaka Indurāja states that Udbhaṭa's तुल्यकाले in the definition by the word तुल्यकाले Indurāja suggests that either it will be Dīpaka nor too wide application rather it would be clearly side.[122]

Udbhaṭa states that the समन्यूनविशिष्टै: in the definition of figure Parivṛtti which is deficient in one respects the word परिवृत्ति in the definition which also means परिवृत्ति itself. Mammaṭa and Ruyyaka used विनिमय in case of परिवर्तन. Indurāja clearly states about the word समन्शूनविशिष्टै: in this figure. He also agrees on the अर्थानर्थस्वभाव of परिवृत्ति said by Udbhaṭa.

GROUP VI

Bhāmaha visualises Sasaṅdeha for the first time, taking it to be सादृश्यमूलक alaṁkāra. Udbhaṭa also follows Bhāmaha in this regard, and calls it as Sasaṅdeha. Rājānaka Tilak, the Vivṛtikāra has the two names for this alyṁkāra, viz. Sandeha and Sasandeha.[123] The later writers call it as Sandeha alaṁkāra.

---

१२१. KASS with Laghuvṛtti, N.D. Banhatti, p. 139.

१२२. सहादिना च शव्देन युगपत्कालतायामवद्योत्यमानायां द्वयी गतिः ।

—इन्दुराज, ल० वृ०, पृ० ७३

१२३. ससंदेहशब्दाभ्यां द्वाभ्यामव्यभिधानमित्युपदेशलक्षरणयार्न विरोधः ।

—राजानक तिलका ल० वि०, पृ० ५०

Udbhaṭa also composed the another alaṁkāra is called Saṅdeha.[124] Vāmana calls these Saṅdeha of Bhāmaha as Saṅdeha.[125]

Ananvaya Alaṁkāra comes from Bhāmaha and Udbhaṭa borrows[126] the same definition from Bhāmaha.[127] Daṇḍin tells it is one of the branches of Upamā and includes in Asādhāraṇe-pamā[128] Later on, it found its own identity. Indurāja explains this alaṁkāra by saying that there is no similarity in उपमेय and उपमान. Indurāja also emphasises the supreme aim[129] of the Ananvaya. असादृश्य रिवक्षा is the basis of Ananvaya to both of Bhāmaha and Udbhaṭa.

According to Bhāmaha संसृष्टि is an important alaṁkāra because it is the mixture of many alaṁkāras and the सौन्दर्यं

---

१२४. अलङ्कारान्तरच्छायां यत्कृत्वाधीषु बन्धनम् ।
असंदेहेपि संदेहरूपं संदेहनाम् तत् ॥
—उद्भट-का० सा० सं० ६.३

१२५. उपमानोपमेयसंशयः संदेहः ।
—वामन, का० सू० वृ० ४ ३ ११

१२६. यत्र तेनैव तस्य स्यादुपमानोपमेयता ।
आ सादृश्यविवक्षातस्तमित्याहुरनन्वयम् ॥
—उद्भट, का० सा० सं० ६.४

१२७. यत्र तेनैव तस्य स्यादुपमानोपमेयता ।
आसादृश्यविवक्षातस्तमित्याहुरनन्वयम् ॥
—भामह, का० अ०, ३.४५

१२८. आत्म नैवाभवत् तुल्यमित्यसाधारणोपमा ।
—दण्डी—का० आ०, २.३७

१२९. नात्रोपमानोपमेयभावे तात्पर्यं किन्तु उपमेयोपमात्रदपमानान्तरव्या-वृत्तावित्यर्थः ॥ —इन्दुराज, ल० वृ०, वर्ग ६

comes out by the combination of many of them.[130] Daṇḍin[131] speaks संस्सृष्टि is the combination of many alaṁkāras and it is of two types.

अंगागीभाव अवस्थित्ति and तुल्यबलता (समकक्षता). The later achāryas take this divisions as the basis of संकर and संसृष्टि अलंकार. But Udbhaṭa's definition[132] indicates the difference of संकर and संसृष्टि clearly.

Bhāmaha takes the Bhāvika to be the Prabaṅdhaguṇa According to him, that Prabaṅdhaguṇa which skilfully enlivens the past or forthcoming meaning of the poet's description, is called Bhāvika (भाविकेत्व) Bhāmaha acknowledges it as a guṇa instead of an alaṁkāra, the directness of Bhāvika is counted as भाविकत्व. Śabdānukūlatā is also included in Bhāvika. According to Daṇḍin, it is a Prabandhaviṣayaka like Bhāmaha. Udbhaṭa establishes it as a Kāvyālaṁkāra to the first time, and termed it as Bhāvika. He adopts the glossary of Bhāmaha with a slight change and among the निष्पादक elements of Bhāvika accepts the अद्भूतता and वाचामनाकुल्य. Further, he eliminates the कधायास्वाभिनीतता, the second constituent of Bhāmaha's definition. Indurāja includes झगित्यर्थ प्रतीतिप्रसाद and अर्थव्यक्तिगुणा in the Bhāvika. In the process of defining the Bhāvika concept of Bhāmaha and Daṇḍin, Indurāja explains Bhāvika with rasa; as "the spontaneous outcome of the sense helps in the profound feeling of the rasa". Bhāvika's such a characteristic facilitates

१३०. वरा विभूषा संसृष्टिर्बह्यलङ्कारयोगतः ।
रचिता रत्नमालेव सा चैवमुदिता यथा ॥

—भामह-का० अ० ३.४६

१३१. नानालङ्कारसंसृष्टिः संसृष्टिस्तु निगदते ॥

—दण्डी, का० आ० २.३५६

१३२. अलङ्कृतीनां बह्वीनां द्वयोर्वापि समाश्रयः ।
एकत्र निरपेक्षाणां मिथः संसृष्टिरुच्यते ॥

—उद्भट, का० सा० सं० ६.५

the reflection of the essence of the poets expression in the hear of the thinker. By taking Bhāmaha's चित्रोदात्ताद्भूतार्थत्वम Udbhaṭa indicates the word वाचामनाकुल्येन which is the real तत of Bhāmaha's भूतभाविनि: view on भाविक explained by Indurāja in the light of philosophical point of view.[133]

According to Bhāmaha, the whole realm of poetic express tion is permited with Vakrokti, striking, deviating expression So as the lack of expression in Hetu he refutes the existence o Hetu in the province of alaṃkāra.[134] But this was acceptec by Daṇḍin. Udbhaṭa speaks the Kāvya Hetu which does no come under the subject of तर्कशास्त्र. This is not the वास्तविकहेतु rather the काव्यात्मक हेतु. Udbhaṭa discusses this Hetu alaṁkāra for the first time in his ending chapter. Udbhata takes the स्मृति and अनुभव words from the logicians. He speaks tha शास्त्रहेतु depends on vision and काव्यहेतु on hearing experience Vāmana and Rudraṭa has not discussed this alaṃkāra. Indurāja details that logicians are rushly and insipidly describe the हेतु but Kāvyahetu has its richness in favour and is intensely appealing to the heart of people by its own composition in poetry which suggests the oppositeness of शास्त्रलिङ्ग is ludicrous (the logical अनुमान inference).

Udbhaṭa introduces the Kāvyadṛṣṭānta alaṃkāra for the first time by adding the view बिम्बप्रतिबिम्बभाव and उपमासूचक पद

---

१३३. एतमनन्तरोपलक्षिताः भूता भाविनश्चभवेर्थास्ते साम्प्रतिकप्रध्वंसाभाव प्रागभावविविक्त तथा वर्त्तमानस्य मानाः प्रत्यक्षा इव यत्र दृश्यन्ते तद्भाविकं नामालङ्कारी भवेत् ।

—इन्दुराज, ल० वृ०, वर्ग-६

१३४. गतोऽस्तमर्को भातीन्दुर्यान्तिवासाय पक्षिणः इत्येवमादि किं काव्यं वार्त्तमेनां प्रचक्षते ।

—भामह, का० अ०, २.८७

अभाव. The figure is called by later ālaṃkārikas by the name of Dṛṣṭānta'. Udbhaṭa discards the यथा, इव ann applies the इष्टस्यार्थस्य विस्पष्ट प्रतिबिम्बनिदर्शनम् in this alaṁkāra. Udbhaṭa speaks it Kāvya Dṛṣṭāntā the purpose behind it is most probably we separates it from the Dṛṣṭānta of Nyāya philosophy. Rudrața classifies it into two types, yiz. विवक्षित and अविवक्षित. Vāmana totally omits this alaṃkāra. Indurāja explains that if इव आदि comes this alaṃkāra then there is the possibility to frame the Upamā. So he appreciates this यथेवादि पदैः शून्यं which already acomodate in Udbhaṭa's definition and the साधारणधर्म is taken in आदि which causes the presence of प्रतिवस्तूपमा.

In this way, the Laghuvṛttikāra explained 41 Alaṃkāras of KĀSS. Though it is not an independent work by the commentator, still it sometimes shows the independent thinking of the Laghuvṛttikāra.

CONCLUSION

An attempt has been made in the foregoing pages t establish Indurāja's contribution to Sanskrit poetics. In cour of analysing the materials of this topic, it emerged as a ver positive and praise-worthy work which embraces his greatne as a whole. It is also significant that Indurāja comments o Udbhaṭa's KASS and apparently borrows Vāmana's views. Th identification of Pratihārendurāja with Bhattendurāja is a sign ficant issue.

Again when the commentary Laghuvṛtti manifes through the work of Udbhaṭa it appears in the form of exhau tive gloss of the Alaṁkāras.

In the first chapter a summary of the Early History c Alaṁkāras has been mentioned upto the advent of Indurāja.

The second chapter gives the general idea of Udbhaṭa personality, life history and works. Among his works onl KASS is availabie, the rest is lost from the horizon of Sanskr Literature. They are known by their names only. Sometime the quotations are available from the lost works.

The available account about the MSS. of KASS i discussed. A resume of KASS with Laghuvṛttl is also mer tioned. The commentators and their expositions about KAS slightly form part of this chapter.

In third chapter the treatment of guna, rasa and dhva in Kāvya as understood by Indurāja has been dealt with i the light of literary analysis.

Along with the advent of the word 'Alaṁkāra' in Sanskr Poetic the six vargas of KASS with Laghuvṛtti by Indurāj forms part of this chapter. This enables to heighten Indurāja' position in the Sanskrit Poetics as a well-known commentator.

The materials available on this topic have been very canty. The different chapters divided in this dissertion are ade with a view to present the work of Udbhaṭa with the ommentary Laghuvṛrti·

A conclusion has been mentioned at the end to bring rth the salient topics and relevant material disussed by me.

Pratiharendurāja made a rich contribution in his lone ommentary by creating a novel genre in the field of rhetories nd by making it a forceful and unexcelled and giving a oroughly analytical treatment of Udbhaṭa in the light of ther prominent Poeticians. Modern scholars willingly accept is greatness because there remains the treasure of unparalleled iscussion and novel exposition of alaṁkāras, guṇa, dhvani, asa etc. with felicitous expresston.

— —

SELECT BIBLIOGRAPHY

Abhidhāvṛttamātṛkā of Mukula Bhaṭṭa, Revā Prasada Dwivedi, The Chowkhamba Vidya Bhawna, Varanasi, 1973.

Abhinavagupta, K.C. Pandey, 2nd Revised edition, Vol. I, The Chowkhamba Sanskrit Series, 1963.

Alaṃkāra Sarvasva, Ruyyaka, R.C. Dwivedi, Motilal Banarasidass, Ist ed., 1965

Amarusataka—Vidyaniwasa Mishra, Ist ed., Raja Kamal Publications, Delhi, 1965.

Aucitya Vicara Carcā, Kṣemendra

Bhaṭṭi Kāvya of Bhaṭṭi, Śri Sesaraja Sharma Shastri, Chowkhamba Sanskrit Series Office, Varanasi, Vikrama Samvat 2007.

Bhoja's Sṛṅgāra Prakāśa, V. Raghavan, Madras 1963.

Comm. of Bhagavad Gitā of Abhinavagupta edited by wasudev Laxman Shastri Pansikar, 2nd ed., Published by Pandurang Jawaji, Nirnaya Sagara Press, Bombay, 1936.

Comm. on Rudraṭa's Kāvyālaṃkāra by Namisādhu

Dhvanyāloka, Ānandavardhana Srisobhit Mishra, Chowkhamba Sanskrit Series Office, Varanasi, 1964.

Dhvanyāloka Locana, Abhinavagupta

Ekāvalī, Vidyādhara

History of Sanskrit Poetics, P. V., Kane, III revised edition, Motilal Banarasidass, 1961.

History of Sanskrit Poetics, S. K. De Firma KLM Private Limited, Calcutta, 1976.

Kāvyādarśa of Daṇḍin, Dharmendra Kumar Gupta, Ist ed., Mehar Chand Laxman Dass, Delhi, 1973.

Kāvyālaṁkāra of Bhāmaha, P. V. Naganath Sastri, IInd ed. Motilal Banarasidass, 1970.

Kāvyālaṃkāra of Rudraṭa Satyadev Chowdhury, Vasudev Prakasana, Delhi, 1965.

Kāvya Mīmāṃsā of Rājśekhar, Kedarnath Sarma Sarsvata, Bihar Rastrabhasa Parisad, Patna, 1954.

Kāvyānuśāsana of Hemachandra, Pt. Sivadatta Kasinath.

Kāvya Prakāśa of Mammaṭa, Sri Hari Sankara Sharma. Vth ed., Chowkhamba Sanskrit Samsthana; Varanasi, 1982.

Kāvyālaṃkāra-sāra-saṃgraha with Laghu Vivṛti of Rājānak Tilak, K. S. Ramasvami Shastri, Gaekwad's Oriental series (GOS), 1931.

Kāvyālaṃkāra-sāra-saṃgraha with Laghu Vṛtti of Praṭihārendu rāja, N. D. Banhatti, Bombay Sanskrit Series, Poona, 1925.

Kāvyālaṃkāra-sāra-saṃgraha of Udbhaṭa with Laghu Vṛtti, R.S. Tripathy.

Kāvyālaṃkāra-Sūtra-Vṛtti of Vāmana, Acharya Visveswar Siddhanta Siromani, Atmarama & Sons, Delhi, 1954.

Mahābhārata, Uddyoga Parva

Nātya Śāstra of Bharata, R. S. Nagara, Ist ed., Parimal Publications, Delhi, Vol. II, 1984.

Nirukta of Yāṣka, V.P. Limaye, Panini, New Delhi; 1982.

Pratāpa Rūdrīya Yaso Bhūṣaṇa of Vidyānātha commentary on Ratnapana, V. Raghavan, The Sanskrit Society, Madras, 1979.

Rājataraṅginī of Kalhaṇa, Ranjit Sitaram Pandit, Sahitya Academy, 1968.

Sāmveda

Subhāsitāvalī, edited by Rama Chandra Malviya, Varanasi, 1974.

Suvṛtta Tilaka—Kṣemendra

Vimaraśinī Tīkā of Jayaratha—R.P. Dwivedi, IInd ed., Chowkhamba Sanskrit Samsthana, V.S. 2036.

Viṣṇudharmottara Purāṇa—Vol. 3, Ksemarāja Srikrsna Dass, Sri Venkateswar Printers, Bombay.

Vyaktiviveka Tīkā.

Secondary Sources

Numbar of Rasas—V. Raghvan.

Outlines of Sanskrit Poetics—G. Vijayavardhana, Chowkhamba Sanskrit Series Office. Varanasi-1, 1970.

Some Concepts of the Alaṃkāra Śāstra—V. Raghavan, The Adyar Library, Adyar, 1942.

Some Problems on Sanskrit Poetics—Sushil Kumar De, Firma K. L. Mukhopadhyaya, Calcutta, 1959.

Studies in Sanskrit Sāhitya Śāstra—V.M. Kulkarni, Ist ed., Bhogilal Leherchand Institute of Indology. Patan, 1983.

The Dhvanyāloka and Its Critics—K. Krishnamoorthy, Ist ed., Kavyalaya Publishers, Mysore, 1968-

Hindi Books

अलङ्कारों का स्वरूप विकास—डा० ओम् प्रकाश, नैशनल पब्लिशिंग हाउस, प्रथम संस्करण, १९७३

अलङ्कार धारणा—विकास और विश्लेषण—डा० शोभाकान्त मिश्र, बिहार हिन्दी ग्रन्थ अकादमी, पटना, प्रथम संस्करण, १९७२

भारतीय काव्यशास्त्र की भूमिका—डा० नगेन्द्र, नैशनल पब्लिशिंग हाउस, नई दिल्ली, तृतीय संस्करण, १९७६

भारतीय काव्यशास्त्र के सिद्धान्त—डा० कृष्णदेव झारी, शारदा प्रकाशन, नई दिल्ली, प्रथम संस्करण, १९८०

भारतीय काव्यसमीक्षा में अलङ्कार सिद्धान्त—डा० रेवा प्रसाद द्विवेदी, दि मैकमलिन कम्पनी आफ इण्डिया लिमिटेड, प्रथम संस्करण १९८०

सरस्वतीकण्ठाभरण का अलङ्कार निरूपण—डा० केदारनाथ शुक्ल, देवनगर प्रकाशन, जयपुर, प्रथम संस्करण, १९८३

संस्कृत अलङ्कारशास्त्र का समन्वित इतिहास—ड० अनिरुद्ध जोशी, अजन्ता प्रकाशन, दिल्ली, प्रथम संस्करण, १९८४

संस्कृत काव्यशास्त्र में व्यावहारिक समीक्षा—देवदत्त कौशिक, भारतीय विद्या प्रकाशन, १९८१

संस्कृत व्याकरण का उद्‌भव और विकास—डा० सत्यकाम वर्मा, मोतीलाल बनारसीदास, १९७१

अभिनन्दन ग्रन्थ

जगन्नाथ तिवारी अभिनन्दन ग्रन्थ—आचार्य हज़ारीप्रसाद द्विवेदी

Dictionaries and Catalogues

Sanskrit-English Dictionary—Vaman Shiv Ram Apte, Motilal Banarasidass, Delhi.

संस्कृत शब्दार्थ कौस्तुभ—संपा० द्वारिकाप्रसाद शर्मा चतुर्वेदी, पं० तारणीश झा, रामनारायण लाल प्रकाशन, द्वितीय संस्करण, १९५७

The New Catalogorous Catalogrum—V. Raghvan.

INDEX